For
Renee + Brian
and
the family

With love,

D0927050

SACRED WOUNDS

SACRED WOUNDS

SUCCEEDING

BECAUSE

OF LIFE'S

PAIN

JAN GOLDSTEIN

ReganBooks

An Imprint of HarperCollins*Publishers*

HarperCollins books may be purchased for educational, business, or sales promotional use. For information please write: Special Markets Department, HarperCollins Publishers Inc., 10 East 53rd Street, New York, NY 10022.

FIRST EDITION

Printed on acid-free paper

Library of Congress Cataloging-in-Publication Data

Goldstein, Jan.
    Sacred wounds: succeeding because of life's pain / Jan Goldstein.—1st ed.
    p. cm.
    ISBN 0-06-009657-8
    1. Conduct of life. 2. Suffering. 3. Success. 4. Goldstein, Jan. I. Title.

BF637.C5 G66 2003
296.7—dc21

2002031625

03 04 05 06 07 WB/RRD 10 9 8 7 6 5 4 3 2 1

For Bonnie,
my best friend
and life's partner.
Your love empowers
the engine
of my dreams.

Je t'aime.

CONTENTS

Introduction   1

Step One: Acknowledging the Wound   23

Step Two: Letting Go of Guilt   43

Step Three: Draining the Profane from the Pain   65

Step Four: Accepting the Wisdom   91

Step Five: Claiming Our Journey   113

Step Six: Honoring the Wound   143

Step Seven: Embracing the Hope   167

Step Eight: Generating the Blessings   191

Step Nine: Transforming Power into Empowerment   213

Epilogue   235

Acknowledgments   239

SACRED WOUNDS

THE LANGUAGE OF PAIN: Why Job Just Didn't Get It

> *There is no coming to consciousness without pain.*
> —Carl Jung

*T*hey say there are only two things in life of which we can be certain—death and taxes. *They* are wrong.

There is a third. Its truth is intensely personal and at the same time universal: along the road of life we will—each and every one of us—*encounter pain.* If we are fortunate it will come and go softly, as in the passing of a loved one who has lived a long and productive life. For many of us, however, pain comes in the form of a difficult childhood, severed relationships, rejection in matters of the heart, physical challenges, personal failure, dismissal in the workplace, serious illness, or the traumatic death of those closest to us.

Pain, hardship, and struggle have been part of the human condition since our lovely orb of earth big-banged into existence. Whether the Garden of Eden is factual or poetic is not the issue here. In the cultural and religious consciousness of the Western world, we were booted out of Paradise and became hardwired to a tempest-tossed universe.

In Genesis, as a consequence of her disobeying a single admonition, the Almighty punishes Eve and, through her, all women, promising to "greatly multiply your pain. . . ." In case we miss the point, it is reiterated: "In anguish shall you bring forth children." This little exchange, with its severe retribution for a seemingly minor infraction, has always struck me as less God the Father than simply the *Godfather*.

Now, men, we've got our own share of dire retribution: "Cursed is the ground because of you" is God's offering to Adam and the testosterone-equipped generations to come; "in toil shall you eat of it . . . thorns and thistles it shall bring forth to you. . . ."

Each time I've pondered this passage, the same disturbing question emerges: exactly why are we condemned with such harshness for eating from the Tree of Knowledge of Good and Evil? After all, isn't the quest for knowledge part of being human?

Maybe the dramatic and divine act of expulsion was simply an excuse. I have a strong suspicion that the idea beneath the story is that we weren't meant to live in Paradise after all. We were meant for the real world, with all of its struggles.

The promise of pain at the very onset of human consciousness is not the sole province of the Western mind. It is a thread that can be detected in ancient cultures and religious traditions from around the world.

- The Mayan creation story, the *Popol Vuh,* or "Council Book," speaks of the Blood Gatherer, one of several "sublords" of Death whose purpose, from the moment of creation, is to afflict ordinary folks.
- The Fulani of Mali in Africa have a creation myth in which Doondari finds that humankind is too proud and as a penalty inflicts its members with blindness and worry.
- In Vedic Hinduism, humanity is seen as susceptible to forces that affect our health, wealth, and loved ones. It is understood that joy and suffering commingle. Early Hin-

dus tried to appease the various gods and stave off suffering with rituals and offerings that eventually came to be understood as symbolic worship.

⚜ In the Mahaparanibbana sutra, Buddha is found in excruciating pain. In fact, while he is still the Hindu prince Siddhartha, his own anguish had inspired him to struggle with the riddle of life: *Why is there so much suffering?* His enlightenment brought about his metamorphosis into the Buddha, and still he experiences pain. The Four Noble Truths of Buddhism begin with the profound acknowledgment: *"All life is suffering."*

Human suffering is so inherent and so mystifying that virtually all cultures and religions seek to explain, understand, even absorb into the religion itself this very basic and unchanging human condition: we will suffer. Even the foundations of modern psychology are built on the recognition that pain is a by-product of our existence in, and interaction with, the world. Each and every one of us, whether we take our cue from religion, cultural myth, or the local tarot reader, encounters difficult times and the anguish that accompanies them at some point in our lives. (Most of us, more than once.) It goes with the territory of living in our human skin, with hearts that can break, bodies that can fail, minds that can despair.

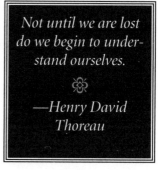

Not until we are lost do we begin to understand ourselves.

❀

—Henry David Thoreau

And yet, there is a silver lining, a gift if you will.

It's there wrapped inside the darkness, waiting only for us to claim it and to build our lives with the beauty of its light. Before we can do so, we have to alter the lenses through which we see, feel, and act. We must come to the realization that life is not so much about attaining happiness as it is about *finding meaning.*

And it is *meaning* that emerges from our inevitable wounds, and *meaning* that we can use to rebuild ourselves into beings capable of more. *We hold the key to turning loss into meaning, meaning into power, and power into success.*

THE MOST FAMOUS BAD LUCK TALE OF ALL TIME

Speaking of loss, let's take just a moment to consider what is, for my money, the most famous bad luck tale of all time, the biblical epitome of faithfulness: God's servant Job.

Job has everything: children in abundance, livestock aplenty, a loving spouse, a diverse portfolio, and loyalty and belief in his Creator by the bucketful. In fact, he's what you might call the poster boy for faith. One fine day, God has justly taken notice of Job, and while in the company of Satan (from the Hebrew word *sathane*, defined as "the opponent"), God says:

> Have you considered My servant Job, that there is none like him on the earth, a blameless and upright man, one who fears God and shuns evil?

But Satan scoffs at Job's blamelessness, and suggests to God a nagging qualifier: it's awfully easy to have a lot of faith when all your ducks are in a row. Why not try judging the man's faithfulness when he's not leading quite so charmed a life? God agrees that Satan has a point, and gives him permission to test Job's faith:

> One day when Job's sons and daughters were feasting and drinking wine at the oldest brother's house, a messenger came to Job and said, "The oxen were plowing and the donkeys were grazing nearby, and the Sabeans attacked and carried them off. They put the servants to the sword, and I am the only one who has escaped to tell you!"

While he was still speaking, another messenger came and said, "The fire of God fell from the sky and burned up the sheep and the servants, and I am the only one who has escaped to tell you!"

While he was still speaking, another messenger came and said, "The Chaldeans formed three raiding parties and swept down on your camels and carried them off. They put the servants to the sword, and I am the only one who has escaped to tell you!"

While he was still speaking, yet another messenger came and said, "Your sons and daughters were feasting and drinking wine at the oldest brother's house, when suddenly a mighty wind swept in from the desert and struck the four corners of the house. It collapsed on them and they are dead, and I am the only one who has escaped to tell you!"

(Job 1:13–19)

What does this virtuous man do as a result of his life having been turned inside out and wrong side up for no apparent reason? Does he threaten legal action? Does he picket the local shepherds' union? Does he sell the rights to his story to expose the rewards of faith in God's topsy-turvy world? Not on your life. Job simply gathers up his ashes, steps out into the street, and raises his fist in contempt. He doesn't cry out at God, the God who possesses the power to protect him but who seems to have cut him loose. He doesn't rail at the injustices of what has suddenly become a cruel and unfeeling universe. He takes all the pain, the anger, and the anguish . . . and turns it against himself.

Yes, Job laments the day he was born:

After this Job opened his mouth and cursed the day of his birth.

And Job said: "Let the day perish wherein I was born, and

the night which said, 'A man-child is conceived.' Let that day be darkness! May God above not seek it, nor light shine upon it.

Job's response to the loss of all he has and all he loves is to strike out at himself and his very existence, and he is nothing if not focused on the task:

Let the stars of its dawn be dark; let it hope for light, but have none, nor see the eyelids of the morning; because it did not shut the doors of my mother's womb, nor hide trouble from my eyes. Why did I not die at birth, come forth from the womb and expire? Why did the knees receive me? Or why the breasts, that I should suck?

(Job 3:1–12)

In fact, what is most notable about Job is that when he finally *does* manage to meet up with the Almighty, who appears in a whirlwind, he folds like a deck of cards. Job doesn't exercise his seemingly justifiable right to know what he has done to deserve such unfairness and suffering; in fact, he apologizes for questioning God's decision to destroy him. And then, in a pièce de résistance of pain internalized, he utters the ultimate words of self-rejection: "*I despise myself.*"

It is this attack upon his own existence that gives me little use for Job as a role model of how to live life in all its challenging glory. In fact, I can't think of anything less healthy or productive than his self-hating response. Job's words and attitude are the same ones we hear and see in today's blessing-filled but demanding world. In response to the pain life throws our way, many of us internalize misfortune and turn it back on ourselves in a self-punishing blitz.

In the wake of great suffering, it is not unusual to inflict guilt upon ourselves and feed our futures with the self-defeating cycles of self-blame. In fact, the word *guilt* comes from the Old English *gylt*, meaning delinquency. When someone carries an unending sense of their own delinquency around with them, there's little chance of forward progress or growth. By playing the blame game, we similarly stunt our future. We allow self-blame and unresolved wounds to fossilize us in a moment from which we seem never able to escape. Such is the path of self-recrimination, of turning pain inward. Like Job's attack upon his own existence, it is a *profane* response to a wound that has not evolved into a *sacred* source of empowerment.

We can do better. We can find meaning.

And we can use that meaning as fuel for personal triumph.

Job certainly could have done better for himself by allowing his wounds to generate self-esteem. He could have used that pain to recognize that blind faith alone does not guarantee happiness. He could have found in his suffering the affirmation that he is nobody's puppet to be manipulated in some strange divine grudge match. He could have used his wounds to create the blessings of renewal necessary to begin again. But he didn't get it. The choice of how to respond to his wounds was his to make. He chose self-punishment, turning the wound upon himself. We can learn from the poor choices of others how *not* to act. Job, for me, makes the all-time poor-choice Hall of Fame.

MASKING THE WOUND

We must, of course, begin by acknowledging the wound itself. This would appear to be a simple matter. After all, if someone we love chooses to leave us, we're brokenhearted. If someone close to us dies, we're bereft. We get laid off from work, we fear for economic security, not to mention the loss of self-esteem. Our wound is there for the entire world to see. Yet how often have we witnessed friends, relatives, and colleagues who have covered their wounds, as Jung would have it, with any number of *masks*?

⚜ The middle-aged, newly divorced woman, traded in for a younger model, hiding her broken heart and loss of pride behind the mask of the workaholic

⚜ The emotionally abused teenager who hides his lacerated spirit behind the facade of a perfectionist while secretly falling into the self-medication of alcohol or drugs

⚜ The adult who has known physical abuse as a child and now uses sexual promiscuity as a means of avoiding authentic human communication

⚜ The spouse of a mate who has suddenly passed away, who pretends at normalcy but, in truth, has simply shut down, withdrawing from life's daily pulse

⚜ Those who use food, status, money, attention, clothes, and jobs to conceal their insecurities

Sound familiar?

WE EACH HAVE OUR STORY

*M*y own wounds go back to a beautiful February morning that quickly became drained of light. At the age of thirty, I was suddenly faced with a divorce and the responsibility of assuming principal physical custody and primary care for my three young children—two daughters, ages eleven and nine, and a son, age six. In all fairness to my wife, and myself, we were married very young. There was a great deal of joy, but also the struggle of literally growing up, even as we took up the mantle of marriage and

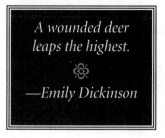

A wounded deer
leaps the highest.

⚜

—Emily Dickinson

parenthood. After a decade, the relationship imploded. My wife said she needed to find her own way, and my life as a single father began.

I stood in my living room as if outside myself, while my wife explained to our children that she was leaving our home. I had known this day was coming ever since she told me of her decision two weeks before. I dreaded this moment, for the children, even as I was experiencing a lightning bolt to the heart from the loss of my marriage. Now I listened to the words that would unalterably change all of our lives.

My wife carefully told our kids how sorry she was, that she knew it was very difficult, but that she needed to leave. She assured them it would all work out all right; they would come for weekly overnights at the apartment she'd arranged. They would speak every day. I know she did her best to explain that life would go on, but information like this is, at best, overwhelming for an adult and even more so for a child.

The air shuddered. Even before her mother had finished her words, my middle child screamed out with a force that would rend the curtain of heaven. The bullet of sound pierced my heart as I witnessed what seemed to me the agony of innocence being torn from her life. My six-year-old son began a singsong babble, not quite comprehending what was happening, or perhaps comprehending all too well and using his own voice to soothe his growing distress. Finally, I focused on the face of my eldest, and my heart came to a complete stop. Her mouth was formed into a gaping wound, emitting absolutely no noise, a silent scream— the loudest and most heartbreaking of my life. As I put my arms out to comfort my children (and no doubt myself as well), I could barely breathe for the pain stifling the room. I remember thinking: how in God's name will we all survive? At that moment in my life I could have been Job's brother, so total was my devastation.

Several days after my wife had left our home, I received an emergency phone call from my sister and flew back to Vermont to be with my father, who had been hospitalized. He had emphysema from many years of smoking, and his heart was giving out. As he lay dying in his hospital bed, he used some of his last words to give me direction.

"*You're getting divorced,*" he whispered. It wasn't a question. Without my having told a single member of my family, he knew.

"*Don't lose the children,*" he warned, with a sudden alertness that shook me to the core. "*Never,*" I promised in hushed reply. "*Be there for them,*" he concluded. It was both a warning and a prayer.

I felt the tearing of my soul as everything came crashing down around me. And at the same time, I also knew what I must do: hold my children. Love them and myself. What I didn't know then, what I couldn't know, was *how* I would do this.

Thus, in the midst of trying to keep my head and the heads of my children above the proverbial waters, life opened the floodgates of suffering. My father died. Suddenly, the man who had always taught through his example how to live a life of love and creativity, who served as my parenting role model, whom I needed now more than ever, was gone.

After the funeral, I returned to my children. They were going through untold grief at the shattering of their family life and the loss of their beloved grandfather. A teacher called me one day to say that it was all simply too much for my children and that I needed to take time to be with them, even if it meant taking a leave from work.

And there was so much more.

Suddenly, I was responsible for every meal. There were doctors' appointments and after-school team practices. Some days all three kids had to be in three different locations at once, while I had to be at the school where I taught or counseling a family in my role as a rabbi. Each night there were three different sets of homework going on as I scrambled from desk to floor to bed, depending on each child's regimen. The mornings were a blur of showers, baths, assembly-line lunches, and fights over who would have the front seat next to Dad en route to school. There was a lot of corner-cutting; racing to the supermarket during my lunch break, cooking late into the night, freezing dinners a week ahead of time. Laundry day consisted of holding a large basket in the hallway between our bedrooms while the children threw clothes from every doorway. We all were coping together, even while our wounds were never far from our hearts and minds.

The toughest times were when the kids got sick; I ran from work to home and back again throughout the day, desperate for a sitter I could trust, crazed with anxiety over leaving a sick child home when I couldn't find one, and finally giving up at work and racing home for good. I coped by taking it one day at a time. I remember the advice of a dear friend who counseled me that, no matter what, the children and I must sit down as a family each night for supper. This would remind the kids that we were still a family unit, and it would provide each of us with an opportunity to talk about our day so that we were all a part of one another's experiences.

The worst times in the first few months weren't when I was schlepping, buying, cleaning, and hustling between work and fatherhood. No. The worst times for me were when I was left alone. I made it a point to drive my kids the thirty round-trip miles to my ex-wife's apartment twice a week because I knew, despite my anger and sense of betrayal, that the children needed their mother. My own mom, freshly widowed, constantly reminded me in our ongoing phone calls that I must refuse to allow my pain to get in the way of what was best for the children.

And so, early on, I would drop them off, kissing them and waving as they disappeared into the apartment complex with their little overnight bags, immigrants from "divorced-family land." I then sat in darkness in my car, down below the apartment window, weeping. The tears were, I know, partly for me. I was, at least for those nights, the odd man out. I missed my family. I missed having a partner. And I was scared, because the next day it would start all over again. At this point, I had no idea how to use my wounds to heal, much less create a new beginning. I only knew that they hurt, and I feared they would simply go on hurting.

There were many nights, in the first few months, when I held my eldest daughter as she lay crying herself to sleep. There were a multitude of painful moments, such as one daughter's discomfort as she had to explain the divorce situation to yet another peer, or eating dinner with an intact family when it was clear my children could see how different their lives had become. So I overcompensated. I would buy extra snacks or tickets to expensive musicals for the whole family. I relied heavily on bagel-and-cream-cheese lunches and tried desperately to conceal from my kids that we were living paycheck to paycheck. At this I know I failed.

Each night, after putting the children to sleep, I would stare up at the stars for a few minutes as if to discern some divine design that would teach me what to do. I began devouring books on divorce, even taking in the movie *Kramer vs. Kramer*, knowing full well it dealt with the pain and challenge of a single father taking over daily child-rearing in the home. I needed catharsis, and I remember sobbing through that film, my wound vibrating with the resonance of my tears. Was there a way out of this pain? Would I wake up one day and find my wounds had finally gone away? Did it work like that? I had no idea.

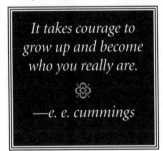

It takes courage to grow up and become who you really are.

—*e. e. cummings*

Over these first few months, however, I was discovering something uplifting. I became aware of the fact that even with my wounds, there were joys present in my life. Cuddling each night with my kids, or taking them for a picnic dinner in the middle of the week just because I could. "We're a creative family," my middle child announced one night when we were returning from a local park where we'd just dined on deli sandwiches and black cherry soda. That tickled me to no end. But for sheer family entertainment, the night I was forced to buy my first bra was, and is, a hilarious moment that gave all of us a needed laugh. It was my middle child, Batsheva, who came to the door of my bathroom as I was shaving to announce that we had to have a little talk. Crossing into my adjacent bedroom, I sat down next to her on the edge of the bed. I was astonished when she informed me that her older sister needed a bra. I insisted that Yaffa was only eleven years old and there did not appear to be, from what I could make out, an immediate cause for concern in that department. My daughter wouldn't budge. Pulling herself up to her full pixie stature, she explained—"My sister is running for student council, and she's going to get up tomorrow in front of the whole school, and she's wearing a white buttoned-down shirt, and it's a little bit, well, kinda see-through, and she needs a bra and that's it!"

I implored her to wait for the weekend and maybe her mother . . . ? It didn't work. Finally, I blurted out in helpless exasperation, "What in the world am I supposed to do?!" My daughter put her hand calmly on my shoulder, reassuring me, "You're the adult, Dad, you'll figure it out." I watched in disbelief as she left the room, confident that her mission was accomplished.

Later that hour, I was banging frantically on the glass of a lingerie store in the mall that had closed only minutes earlier, insisting I needed a bra and I needed it now! The look on the elderly proprietor's face was priceless. She opened the door, in some consternation, asking me for the size. I explained that it was for my eleven-year-old. She said something about a "training bra," and I remarked, "You mean you have to *train* for something like that?"

But in spite of the delights and surprising humor we experienced, I still felt the weight of my wounded spirit and a sense that I would pass on a legacy of loss. I tried telling myself that it was time the pain ended. It was as if I thought I could "will" my suffering away and start a new chapter in life.

But the wounds continued to ache within me. There were reminders everywhere of what we had once been. When I saw a mom and dad together with their kids eating in a restaurant, I would wonder how the image would impact my children. I would feel a tug inside me when the children and I were watching TV and an advertisement for family vacations aired, with its images of a happy family tumbling together in the snow. My guilt over what seemed like *my* failure to keep the family intact ate away at me. What I neglected to see at the time, however, was that the guilt and self-blame robbed me of the energy I needed to help our new family unit to heal and grow. I would lie awake at night, getting very little sleep, then get up early and sit in a hot bath while I tried to figure out how I'd move us all through another day. I began reading about emotional pain in both psychology books and spiritual tomes. I had long sessions with a therapist, as well as with other single moms (at the time I didn't know one single father who had primary custody of his children).

It was after one of my son Elisha's T-ball games that I experienced what I can only call an epiphany. Many families were gathered to cheer on their boys. The girls and I were hooting and hollering in support of their brother. Suddenly, I heard a loud fight breaking out in the stands, and I turned to witness a husband and wife going at each other at the top of their lungs. I realized everyone else, the spectators, the players, my daughters, were all privy to the pain of this couple. And I remember thinking, "Thank God my kids aren't experiencing that between their mother and me!"

Later, when we were all enjoying a postgame ice cream cone, I became acutely aware of the smiles and giggling of my own children. I realized that our pain had somehow allowed us to enjoy moments like this with a deeper appreciation than I could have imagined. I had a feeling of thanksgiving that I had not felt before. Perhaps my wounds were not some profane festering of failure in my life, I thought. What if, in their ability to teach me through experience and instruct me in what matters, my wounds were actually *sacred*?

I began to think about my emotional injuries and listen to

what they had to teach me. I also became aware that I was consciously blessing the experience of my life at the end of the day, thankful for being shown that my children and I possessed a deeper capacity to love. I actually could hear this voice welling up deep within me, urging me to go further, to find what else I had learned. I would record the sentiments this voice conveyed to me, often in the middle of the night. Was it my father's voice, my mother's, my own? It was passionately instilling confidence, assuring me that I was exactly what my children needed. It was telling me I could be strong and creative, like my dad had been. And it reminded me, particularly when I was very down, that I wasn't alone. I was lucky—I had my children.

I became more attentive as a father. If it came down to a choice between family or job, I didn't hesitate. I *listened* more, to my children and to my own heart. And I *heard* more as well. I looked for ways in which we could grow, as individuals and as a family. In addition to the picnics in the middle of the week and the theater outings, we began putting on our own shows before bedtime. The musical *Annie* was popular back then, and the kids and I would take on some of the characters, performing showstoppers as a postdinner activity. Our theatrics became so successful that the kids' friends would come over once a week for special "paper bag" skits. I would fill up bags with all kinds of kitchen utensils and other gadgets, and the children would have to use their imagination to create a play using them. This beat television anytime. Car rides to and from school became *Les Misérables* sing-alongs, and often we would celebrate Friday night Shabbat dinners by lighting candles from a perch above the ocean.

I began to learn to let go of heartache in favor of hope. I would write down the most painful of my experiences and, on the nights my children weren't with me, I would burn them; this became a ritual that allowed for the release of anger and self-guilt. I took to meditating in the warmth of the shower and jogging for my health. I began to write and found that writing

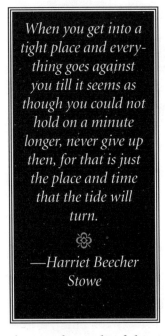

*When you get into a
tight place and every-
thing goes against
you till it seems as
though you could not
hold on a minute
longer, never give up
then, for that is just
the place and time
that the tide will
turn.*

—Harriet Beecher
Stowe

brought a creative energy to my life. I finished a musical on the changing roles of men and women, found a backer, and opened the show in Los Angeles. I then watched in gratitude as my children's excitement for my own enthusiasm grew exponentially. I discovered that if I nurtured my own soul, I actually had more soul to nurture my children.

I began consciously blessing parts of my life with spontaneous prayer. I would pause after saying good night to each of the children and say a silent thank-you for the gift of their lives. I placed my hands on their heads once a week, speaking out loud my hopes and dreams for each of them. I started prioritizing goals in a journal, and at the dinner table, outlining for my kids the values in which I believed: family, self-worth, optimism, creativity, and celebrating the moment. My rituals of letting go and fashioning priority lists, my daily blessings, my meditation, writing, and setting time aside for personal and family growth, allowed me to see my wounds of loss and rejection in a new light. They were beginning to speak to me, not as enemies but as friends. I stopped holding them at arm's length and found myself welcoming their message of renewal and strength.

AN UNEXPECTED POWER

Of course, I would have preferred that life kept its pain to itself. But if the story of Job has taught us anything it's that life is never as neat or considerate as we'd like. I came to see that pain, while never desirable, is capable of producing an unexpected power and inspiring in all of us the potential to grow well beyond where we were before the wounding experience. If we hold our wounds in the core of our souls, alive and sacred, we can use them to shape not only who we want to be but who we were *meant* to be.

As a young child growing up in Vermont, I had a brief but lasting introduction to this kind of human triumph when I had the good fortune to be introduced to the force of nature that was Maria von Trapp. *The Sound of Music,* of course, is based on her life. Her family had fled Nazi Austria and settled in my home state. By the time we met, she could no longer "climb every mountain" or "follow every rainbow," and she also looked nothing like Julie Andrews, a fact I pointed out to her in the manner of small kids who don't know when to keep quiet. She pointed out to me that while she might be old, she was still very young. When I found this puzzling, she told me I would figure it out one day.

One morning, Maria introduced me to a grove of beautiful birch trees to which she regularly escaped for meditation and private singing. Suddenly, she cried out as if a child had fallen. The branch of one of her beloved trees had been struck by lightning and was hanging off the trunk literally by a thread of wood. I was surprised at her grief and watched in wonderment as she stroked the drooping limb the way you might a loved one. Then, as if by magic, a smile appeared on her face. "It has suffered, poor thing, but it will not die." She turned to me. "In a little while, it shall grow even stronger."

A wounded soul is a bit like that branch. We own the power of a second life in which our strength can be restored. As with alchemy, our pain is melted into meaning, and the meaning can be transformed into successful

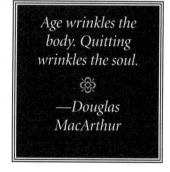

Age wrinkles the body. Quitting wrinkles the soul.

—Douglas MacArthur

and purposeful living. Such is the strength and power of an integrated soul, a soul that transforms wounds into the material of
growth.

COMMUNITY WOUNDS

𝒫ain is not only an individual matter. There are moments in our
lives when a wound is shared by an entire community. As this
book was being completed, the entire world was shaken by the
events of September 11, 2001, when terrorists brazenly comman-
deered commercial airplanes, flying them into the World Trade
Center and the Pentagon. The families of firefighters, medical
workers, police personnel, and ordinary citizens were, and are
still, devastated. The city of New York has experienced the ravages
of personal tragedy. An entire country has been wounded in
spirit and heart, and the world has suffered a direct hit to its collective consciousness. The horrific pain of that day will continue
to evolve and its repercussions will be felt over many years. The
suffering has been most earth-shattering for those closest to the
victims. But this pain has been shared, emanating in concentric
circles, by a nation and a world.

The president of the Czech Republic, Vaclav Havel, an author,
artist, statesman, and one of the world's most acclaimed leaders
of social conscience, knew the terror of suffering imprisonment
for his political beliefs under the Communists, but went on to
lead his nation to freedom. President Havel communicated with
me personally on the subject of our collective wound of September 11, 2001:

> I perceive what happened, first and foremost, to be a
> tremendous warning to all mankind. I think it is necessary,
> in the light of the latest events, to reflect anew and to do
> everything within our power so that human responsibility
> will go hand in hand with human creativity, offering even

great technical possibilities to the good as well as to the bad. The recent events are a great challenge, but not only to reflect upon. It is our duty to do everything possible so that people, their liberty, human rights, democracy and love of life do not become hostages of evil and violence.

As a community, we can rebuild and find meaning, not simply by going about our business and attempting normalcy, but by taking the opportunity to renew our purpose *as* a community in light of our communal Sacred Wound. As with individuals, a collective can succeed only by going *step by step*.

THE NINE STEPS OF REBIRTH

*F*or me, coming to the realization of my Sacred Wounds was truly a rebirth. The nine steps of this book correspond to the nine months in which life develops. The understanding and claiming of our Sacred Wounds unleashes a renewal that truly blesses us with a fresh start in life. When we embrace that "rebirth" by transforming pain into gain, we become our best personal destiny.

Let me say to those among you who are still deep in the darkness of your wounds—there is illumination ahead. To those of you who have some distance from events, the wound within you is yearning to share its light. You may not be ready for all the learning in the pages and days ahead or be able to recognize all the gifts. But what you will surely find is that at each step in the process of your growth, this book will read differently. You may find a word here or a task there that speaks to you with particular clarity. At the moment it grabs you, the learning has begun. Travel with it. Let it stimulate you, your thinking, your perspective, both creatively and spiritually.

If we are wounded, broken by sickness, shattered by the loss of love, torn by doubt, damaged by the workplace, injured by insensitivity to our needs and abuse to our hearts . . . there is a power awaiting us. Just as we feel the impact of life's blows, a form of dying within us, there exists at the same time the paradox of new possibilities being born. When the hammer of life cracks open our hearts and our protective shell lies broken and gaping, it not only allows for our hurt to pour out, but also light to pour in. Cursing our existence when we suffer life's wounds, as Job did, will get us nowhere. He didn't get it, but we can.

In this book, we will learn how to claim our wounds:

- ❀ We will explore the ways in which we can both honor and bless the pain we feel.
- ❀ We will share the inspirational stories of individuals who have absorbed life's difficulties and extracted knowledge and personal power. We will see that their success has come not *despite* their suffering but *because* of it.
- ❀ We will recognize that it is necessary to integrate our wounds into the fabric of our lives, because we can never obliterate them. We will come to see that we need to use them positively, or they will fester and turn inward.
- ❀ We will lay the groundwork for seeking the *sacred* in the midst of the *profane*, and find ways to harness that sacred energy to generate passionate and purposeful living.
- ❀ And we will celebrate the spiritual wholeness that emerges when we integrate our Sacred Wounds into our human hearts.

We will explore each of the nine steps that will move us toward purposeful living and success. Each step will begin with a meditation welcoming the lesson of life's wounds. We will continue our journey through a soul-affirming story illustrating how one acquires power and direction out of personal pain. Finally, we will conclude each chapter with a concrete exercise known as *The Task*, a ceremony called *The Ritual*, celebrating the step, and a coda called *The Gift,* acknowledging the "miracles of self-knowledge" we have gained for ourselves. Taken together, each step will point us toward our own Manifesto for Success, a sanctification and celebration of who we are, wounds and all.

This is the quest we are on: a journey to wholeness. There is no one holding a stopwatch. There is no right or wrong timetable. Go at your own speed and with your own unique sensibility. You can do this. You *can.* You are taking part in the miracle of how human beings find their way. Had Job understood that, he might not have been so dependent on God for *all* of his blessings; he might have seen that he had the power to create his own. How we choose to live between the moments of our birth and death is just that—*our choice.*

The journey of a thousand miles begins with one step.

—*Lao-tzu*

Hold this much in your heart:

> **The path we take is sacred . . .**
> **The journey we take is shared . . .**
> *We are our own best destiny.*

STEP ONE

ACKNOWLEDGING THE WOUND: A Voice from Within

In a dark time, the eye begins to see.
—Theodore Roethke

*W*e begin each step with an original meditation from my heart to yours. I encourage you, throughout this process and beyond, to compose or find additional meditations that speak to your spirit and to your wounds.

THE MEDITATION
Open my eyes that I might see clearly.
Open my ears that I might hear the truth.
Open my mouth that I might speak wisdom.
Let me tell my wounds I will not silence them.
They my spirit will embrace.
Bless my head and bless my journey
With the gift of grace.

I am here . . .
Present in the moment . . .
Ready to begin.

A wound is a living entity. We know this because the effects of the wound produce pain in our lives, activating our physical, emotional, and spiritual centers. By reading this meditation, you have taken the first step toward hearing and attempting to understand what your wounds may be trying to tell you.

THE BIRTH OF A WOUND

*T*here are myriad messages and incidents that can induce suffering:

- ❁ *"Daddy told me I'd never be pretty..."* can produce a wound of inadequacy about one's looks and abilities that can last a lifetime.
- ❁ *"He died before I could tell him I loved him. That fight was the last exchange we had..."* produces a wound of self-inflicted guilt and recrimination.
- ❁ *"You're a loser. You've always been a loser. Why I married you I'll never know..."* produces a debilitating wound to our sense of self-worth.

One may not reach the dawn save by the path of the night.

—*Kahlil Gibran*

These traumas do not go away by themselves. In fact, they often become so overwhelming that they take over our lives, causing us to lose sleep, lose weight, gain weight, drink more, withdraw, abuse those we love, let others down, let ourselves down, and sometimes descend into bitterness, scornfulness, and rage. These wounds take up permanent residence in our soul, and even those people who are part of our distant past continue to play an active and toxic role in our lives.

Along with being a father and an educator, I have served for many years as a rabbi in Los Angeles. I was once officiating at a wedding, looking into the faces of a couple who were clearly filled with the love and celebration of the moment. Suddenly, the bride let out a painful cry, weeping hysterically. She and her sister had been in a car accident when they were teenagers. The sister died. The bride, who had been haunted by the question of why she had lived while her sister had perished, was overwhelmed with guilt at the moment of her greatest joy. After a few moments, and with the support of a very understanding groom, the bride composed herself and the wedding continued. Her wound will always be part of those wedding memories.

Sometimes we listen to our wounds because we can't ignore them. The hurt, the sadness, the anger, the cry from within are all too close to the surface to block out. We'll be looking at pictures of former loves, of deceased family members, of happier times in our lives, and the wound's voice whispers, *Remember me? Remember how I came to be? I'm still here.*

Because we don't want to be reminded of this pain, many of us will try to silence the wound, to ignore its insistent call.

- We get rid of the offending photographs that stir the poison of our pain.
- We move away from the home in which we lived with our lovers or spouses, believing we won't be reminded of them anymore.
- We flee the hometown in which we were raised in order to put distance between ourselves and our families.
- We gorge ourselves on food, liquor, or drugs to silence the wound with addiction.
- We sleepwalk our way through myriad sexual trysts, staying as briefly as possible so as not to be touched too deeply.
- We push people away from us during a serious illness lest we be reminded of all we may lose.

Of course, none of this works. We *will* be reminded, we *will* return to our pain, our wounds will *not* be silenced. This is the presiding principle of Step One.

PAIN IS A PRESSURE COOKER

*I*ndeed, trying to keep our hurt buried, forcing it down deep within us, thinking that we can choke it off through denial and deception, requires so much of our energy that we often have little left for actual living. We might succeed for a brief time in keeping the lid on our wounds, but, like steam in a radiator, the pressure builds. Pressure in a car radiator doesn't affect just one part of the automobile; it brings the entire vehicle to a standstill. This idea reminds me of an acquaintance of mine who made up his mind to ignore his wife's affair. He was not going to allow it to affect him. The man threw himself into his work with ferocity, keeping his emotions in tight check, and within six months, he had a heart attack. We will never know if this attack of the heart was incontrovertibly connected to his personal pain, but it certainly gives one pause, doesn't it?

Samuel Johnson noted: "Adversity is the state in which man most easily becomes acquainted with himself, being especially free of admirers then." But our wounds are not an excuse to shrivel up and withdraw from life. Even if we are alone with our pain, we are being offered the opportunity to learn more about our own hearts and hopes and humanity.

Wounds need to be recognized as part of who we are, because anything less is subterfuge. A life of truth cannot be built on denial and lies. Our painful experiences are part of our uniqueness. Once they've occurred, we can never be truly ourselves without them.

To be human, to be in touch with our authentic selves, is to hear and acknowledge the language of pain as it speaks within us. We can hear it in our heartache over broken relationships, in the fear we feel as a result of serious illness, in our insecurity because of emotional or physical abuse, or in the anguish and numbness over the traumatic loss of a loved one. Sigmund Freud suggested that we typically respond to these feelings of anxiety, fear, and pain through *defense mechanisms,* such as *denial, displacement, projection,* and *rationalization.* In order to assess the extent to which we acknowledge our wounds, we might ask ourselves a few questions:

❀ Do we ever pretend our pain has never occurred or keep it locked up in the recesses of memory, never to be discussed or acknowledged? In other words, is there an element of *denial* in the way we deal with our wounds?

❀ Do we, as a result of repressing our wounds, ever *displace* onto another person our anxiety and anger and fear? A child might get hit by another and come home and strike his sister. Who or what might we be striking out at?

❀ Do we find ourselves *projecting* our wounds onto others by negatively judging their behavior, judgments that rightfully belong with our own feelings of pain? A friend tells me she was out on a postdivorce date, ready to start anew, and she ended up dumping her anger at her ex-husband all over the unsuspecting gentleman she was with. Upon whom do we project our pain?

❀ In not being willing to accept our own suffering, do we ever *rationalize* it, expressing sentiments such as: "Getting physically abused is a fact of life, first as a child and now in my marriage . . . at least I'm being honest about it."

We'll return to these questions in *The Task* at the end of *Step One,* at which point we will be able to make use of the insights we've achieved in the pages to follow.

Before we can use our wounds to heal ourselves, before we can even contemplate the road to accomplishment that a wounded

The beginning of wisdom is to call things by their right names.

✿

—Chinese proverb

spirit offers us, we must first stop our attempts to silence its voice or declare it irrelevant. Calling a wound irrelevant is like calling taxes irrelevant. We might not like the fact that we have to pay them, but they do serve a purpose.

These physical, emotional, and spiritual wounds that we carry with us are life's way of quantifying our suffering. They place their "notch" in our soul, becoming part of our spirit. But when we open our senses to the pain, the messages we hear are the insightful experiences from which we can draw. It's as if we have a teacher within us waiting to be heard. Acknowledging this presence allows the wound to offer itself as a resource for positive change.

———

I have a story to share with you about a woman who managed to reshape her life. She never knew she had that potential until she acknowledged her wounds. In doing so, she set in motion a chain of events that lifted her to a whole new level of existence, allowing her to embrace all she was truly meant to be.

Debrah's Story

*I*f you are looking for a formula for failure, you'd be hard-pressed to find a more suitable example than that of Debrah. As she says, "I didn't miss much on the downhill slide." Her life experience reads like a shopping list for heartache. Tormented by her father, unprotected by a mother who was in denial at the time, Debrah became a high school dropout, and by her thirties, she had passed through three unsuccessful marriages. She was a victim, both as a child and later in her marriages, of physical and emotional abuse, and turned to alcoholism to escape her pain.

Add to that list ovarian and uterine cancer and a near-death car crash in which a motorcyclist put her into a coma for three weeks, and you begin to get the picture of her hardships. They were positively biblical.

Job, my good fellow, move over!

With this kind of experience, Debrah could barely be expected to help herself, much less others. But she had two things going for her: good friends and her young son from her second marriage, who witnessed the darkness of his mother's world and yet loved her with abundance.

Debrah had been a drinker since she was a teenager. Escaping from the physical and emotional abuse she had experienced at the hands of her father, her mother's unwillingness or inability to help her, and the subsequent divorce of her parents, she escalated rapidly into alcoholism. But in her own words, "I was a high-functioning drunk. I could drink heavily at business lunches and still draw up an ad for the newspapers that knocked people's socks off. I worked hard and managed to make a lot of money."

By 1985, Debrah had survived cancer and three marriages, and she had used her characteristic energy to establish a position for herself as vice-president of marketing with a major real estate firm in Los Angeles. She planned the advertising campaigns, conceived the publicity, managed an office staff, and kept right on functioning, alcohol and all. With her high salary, she was able to afford tuition for a Montessori school for her son, Gideon. She even "managed" her drinking, not taking up the bottle until her child was asleep.

People loved her. She had passion. She always knew how to solve business and creative problems and assign roles for a marketing campaign. But the drinking escalated, and one day her ability to hold it all together came to an abrupt and lifesaving stop.

It was the day of her sister's wedding; a glorious moment of family celebration that was suddenly destroyed when Debrah, having tanked up with drinks before and after the ceremony, suddenly created a scene. Boisterously toasting her sister and her new husband, she began spouting nonsensical language, spewing profanities, and finally, with drunken cackles of laughter, raced off with another guest, leaving her anguished twelve-year-old son and angered sister behind.

Soon after this dramatic event, her sister spoke to the therapist Debrah had been seeing, and the two of them confronted her in an intervention. She was an alcoholic, they told her. She had shamed her family and hurt her son. She had to get help.

It was a wake-up call in the middle of the dark side of her life, the one she hadn't really wanted to recognize. "I looked in the mirror as if I were looking at myself for the first time. I hurt from being abused. People I had loved had cut me loose and left me unprotected. On top of it I had faced cancer as a single mom worrying about my son. I'd been beaten up, and I'd been silencing my hurt with alcohol for so long I could've drowned in it."

For the first time in her many years of drinking, Debrah connected the word *alcoholic* with her own wounds of physical and emotional abuse. She finally knew what she had become and she wanted out of the cycle of pain, both for herself and for her son. Leaving him with a close friend, Debrah checked into a month-long rehabilitation program for addiction.

When she came out of the hospital, Debrah began attending daily Alcoholics Anonymous meetings. She was also fortunate to be welcomed back to work by her employer. Her son knew she loved him, but over the years he had witnessed more than she knew. Only her commitment to staying sober and rebuilding trust would convince him that their life together could be secure.

Debrah had begun. She had *acknowledged her wounds*, the first step to her rebirth and renewal. And in committing herself to a different way of life, without the alcohol and subterfuge of late-night drinking, she would come to see that her wounds could elevate her life by giving her new choices. They could become Sacred Wounds.

With all her failures, Debrah had always been both a fighter and a giver. As a little girl, she was known to speak out when things weren't fair. She defended her classmates, and as a young teenager donated her Christmas gifts to those less fortunate.

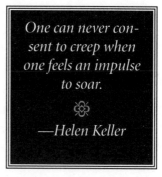

One can never consent to creep when one feels an impulse to soar.

—*Helen Keller*

Debrah had lost herself. But she was about to rediscover her strength and her sense of giving in order to fight her way back and transform not only her own life but ultimately the lives of others.

Within months of becoming sober, Debrah asked to take charge of her real estate company's community affairs department in order to respond to local needs. "I had seen the movie *Stand and Deliver*, about Jaime Escalante, an inner-city teacher," she told me. "Then I read a full-page story about gifted teachers in South Central L.A. who were teaching advanced-placement courses without pay. I figured we might be able to underwrite and enlarge the program. I asked my boss why we were giving our company funds to affluent schools in Brentwood when we could be doing something important in the inner city. He said, 'Go do it, Debrah.'"

She contacted the advanced-placement chemistry teacher running the program, Roland Ganges. His response was so unexpected, it stopped her dead in her tracks. "Thank you," he said, "but I don't want your money. What I need is your time."

Debrah couldn't fathom what he was talking about: "I said, 'Great, the man is a nut case. I mean, what could beat hard cash when you wanted to get something done?'" Nevertheless, Mr. Ganges pressed her to come to South Central and meet the children with whom he was working. Though puzzled, Debrah consented. On her way to this disadvantaged area, she got nervous. Why would this teacher want her time? "My God," she thought, "I don't even have a high school education. What could I possibly be able to do to help these students?"

And then she arrived in South Central, and what she found there not only touched her heart, it changed her life.

"I saw all these children excited by what Roland Ganges and the others were doing—they were opening possibilities for them! Kids were challenging one another with theories I couldn't make heads or tails out of. The classroom was filled with hands waving like crazy, it was like a carnival. Only this stuff they were learning about would take them somewhere. It would take them to tomorrow."

Ganges explained to Debrah that the kids in his school did not have balance in their lives. They were poor. They never went anywhere. They needed exposure to the outside world, beyond the borders of the neighborhood. And they needed to learn about giving back. Could she help him?

Winston Churchill once said, "I never worry about action, only inaction." Debrah was of a similar mind. The receptive and eager faces of the children wanting to learn and grow, surviving in what was nothing short of a battle zone, shook a voice free inside of her. "I'd been through cancer, close to death, addicted to alcohol, lived through abuse. I thought I'd seen it all. But seeing these kids, the hope but also the poverty, the fact that they didn't even always have enough food, it just all seemed so unfair."

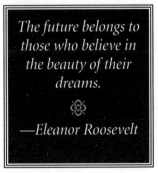

The future belongs to those who believe in the beauty of their dreams.

—Eleanor Roosevelt

Her wounds reminded Debrah that she had lived in her own battle zones, just like these kids. She—who had felt the rape of her spirit in her father's punishing blows—knew better than anyone what awaited these children if they were truly destined to a life ruled by violence and despair. Her own history with her wounds had taught her that life is not simply about claiming victory over despair for yourself, it is about using that triumph to help others know that they can also survive and succeed. Pain has a purpose, she thought. It can propel me forward and help me to help others.

It was at that moment that she first glimpsed what living one's own truth, being one's own authentic person, could do. It was at that moment that Debrah understood the premise and purpose of Sacred Wounds.

Debrah came up with a brilliant program that paired students with volunteers from her company. Side by side, a child from South Central and an adult from her office in Beverly Hills fashioned a bond. They gathered blankets for the homeless, assisted the elderly with chores around the house, and worked together on the fund-raisers Debrah arranged through charities in the area. Debrah was inspired by the success of the program, and set out to convince other companies to help make a difference with the students.

One day a friend asked her a question that unlocked the answer Debrah needed to unleash her true potential: "What do you really want to do with your life?" Debrah paused. It seemed a simple enough question, yet it caught her by surprise. "No one has ever asked me that before," she said. And then, without another thought, like a dam bursting, she heard herself blurt out in one long, life-affirming breath: "I want to open a safe house in South Central where the students can go after school to get off the dangerous streets, where they can get a healthy snack, a pat on the back, maybe a hug; where they can get a chance to do their homework; and where someone will be there to tell them that what they're doing is special, that they are special."

For so much of her own life, Debrah had not felt secure. Danger—physical abuse, emotional abuse, parental neglect, her own and others' alcoholism—had always lurked in the corners of her life where she had kept her wounds, silent and out of sight. Now it was in acknowledging these wounds that Debrah found the courage to pursue her deepest wish.

Six months later, Debrah, with one volunteer and a small budget, brought A Place Called Home into being. Her safe house began in three rooms of a church amid streets often marked by gang wars. Debrah had convinced the local priest that she had the passion and the drive to see it through. "He looked at me like I was a bit crazy," she told me, "but, hey, not much else was working in the neighborhood in terms of after-school programs." Having saved money from the lucrative job she'd held in Beverly Hills, Debrah had enough for her son and herself for the time being. Gideon expressed his support for his mom's new venture, and every night Debrah had new stories to share with him, building their bond.

Twelve children showed up that first day in the fall of 1993—a dozen kids who were willing to agree to the terms of Debrah's simple but essential contract that prioritized safety in her new fledgling program: *no weapons, no drugs, no alcohol, no graffiti,* and *no bigotry.* Those who wished to participate had to sign this contract and abide by it. Just one violation and you were gone—period.

Slowly at first, but with increasing frequency, the original twelve participants brought siblings and convinced a few friends to drop by. By word of mouth the news spread among the gangs and in the neighborhood. What Debrah was doing was working. The safe house was gradually, but most definitely, *happening.* As for Debrah: "Seeing the children thrive, hearing the laughter instead of what was out in the streets, I knew then that this was what I was meant to do."

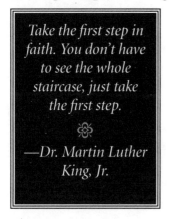

Take the first step in faith. You don't have to see the whole staircase, just take the first step.

—Dr. Martin Luther King, Jr.

With the numbers of children enrolled in her program inching up steadily, Debrah managed to attract corporate and private sponsors to help fund the program. She was putting wings on her dream, but it was not without struggle. Debrah knew there was one outreach effort she hadn't yet tried and couldn't avoid. During her brief tenure in South Central, she had learned that the children were often faced with a dangerous choice: the street or the playground, both of which were penetrated by the aggression of the gangs.

She had to approach the gangs directly. She wasn't going to be able to end the cycle of violence that had terrorized the neighborhood, she told herself. But she might convince one or two of the gang members to join her program and then, who knows? Again, her wounds spoke to her. She knew she had already been to hell and back, and there was nothing left to fear. She decided to be patient and wait for the right moment to present itself . . . and she didn't have long to wait.

One December day, a fight broke out in front of the safe house's church. Uzis were drawn, one gang pitted against another. Seeing some of her children on their way to A Place Called Home out in the middle of the warfare, she rushed to them. Standing between the opposing groups, Debrah held up her arms and shouted, "Some of you people I've seen in our center. I know you want the Christmas party coming up, the presents, the fun. There is going to be nothing unless these guns are put away. Now." Debrah wasn't afraid. Her Sacred Wounds produced an inner power and calm that allowed her to take the action she felt necessary.

One of the leaders, a combat veteran in his teens named Miguel, was so taken aback he didn't know whether to laugh or pull the trigger. No one had ever spoken to him like that or dared ask him to put down his gun. Here was a white woman in the middle of a black and Latino neighborhood. A *white* woman! He'd seen church leaders, youth volunteers, the occasional white do-gooder down in the 'hood before. None of them had ever impressed him, they didn't come near him, and he avoided them. But he had to admit that this woman was doing something different with some of his fellow gang members in this program of hers.

Sometime after that day, Debrah broke up another fight. Miguel was there again with his gang. Debrah approached him, a look of determination in her eyes. Unafraid. She asked him for his gun. He remembers: "I mean, she had the *cojones* to ask me, one of the gang members everybody was scared of, me, she asks for my gun. So, what could I do? We all thought she was this tough lady who was doing some good for the people, you know, so . . . I gave it to her."

A few months later, after Debrah had moved her growing program to a larger facility in South Central, Miguel came up to see Debrah and asked for a job. "I told him he'd have to agree to give up his gun and go to therapy," Debrah recalls. "He'd also need to go into a program for drug and alcohol abuse. He agreed. He has become like another son. He is my hero."

The first time I met Miguel, I was in for a stunning introduction. I asked him how his life had changed since he'd come to A Place Called Home. He simply lifted up his shirt and pointed to the six bullet wounds that dotted his chest. "This was my future," he said, "until I met Debrah."

Today, A Place Called Home gathers together several hundred nine- to twenty-year-olds each day for its programs, providing both a supportive and safe atmosphere and a reason to believe in themselves. Debrah wanders from room to room, shouting a string of encouragements, giving a hug here, some tough love there. The facility exists like an island of sanity and care in the midst of barbed-wire bedlam. Debrah oversees a staff of forty-four and an annual budget of $2.3 million. The children and teens take part in art and dance lessons, record their music in a state-of-the-art studio, fashion dolls out of yarn, learn kickboxing, write poetry, tap away at computers. And each of them, every last one of them, has forsworn weapons and drugs in this still-blighted area. A Place Called Home is the only building the gangs respect enough to place it off limits from "tagging" or vandalism of any kind.

As Marina, a woman who saw her three children flourish at A Place Called Home, explains: "Sometimes it only has to take one person to change a life. For us, that person is Debrah."

And it all came from the heart and soul—and Sacred Wounds—of one woman. Torn by life in so many ways, she mended the breach within. Acknowledging and listening, finally, to her wounds, she answered with healing. Hearing the pain, she learned to use its message to inspire her creative spirit. A woman who couldn't make it through the twelfth grade had come to offer the education of a lifetime by teaching that *the past doesn't equal the future* and *pain can be the birthplace of hope.*

Three years ago, Debrah Constance and the program she created were hailed by President Clinton's Summit on Youth as "one of the fifty best teaching examples in America." Corporate organizations like Viacom and HBO regularly employ interns from her programs. Among the thousands who send donations and come by to volunteer, supporters such as comedian Johnny Carson, columnist Arianna Huffington, and actor Will Smith have applauded what she has accomplished.

Recently Debrah shared with me her grateful satisfaction in having just completed her sixteenth year of sobriety. Speaking of her past wounded spirit and the mission she now feels, Debrah radiates passion: "Seeing these kids, it's like heaven—nothing makes me happier than to take hard-core gang members and turn them around. The gang members in this neighborhood are either going to prison or they will be killed. I'm in a race to beat that deadline. Coming to terms with my wounds has meant acknowledging and believing in myself. It has also meant learning to believe in others. I believe in these kids." Debrah's son, Gideon, has become a doctor. Her protégé Miguel is working as a gang-prevention counselor in a neighborhood program. Debrah continues leading her island of affirmation in the middle of South Central, making sure not only to acknowledge the wounds of those around her, but, most important, their dreams as well.

———

Debrah's wounds also allowed her to see more clearly the very real struggle of others, and they became the source of inspiration and strength to do something for herself and for others. She embodies *Step One*, for it was in her acknowledgment of her wounds that she began to merge her pain with personal possibility, creating a pathway to her own healing and elevating her soul's purpose. This is what I mean when I call life's suffering "Sacred Wounds."

As Marcel Proust observed: "We are healed of a suffering only by experiencing it to the full." When we acknowledge our wounds, we take the most important *First Step* toward healing and success.

———

THE TASK

Find a safe, comfortable place, and set aside thirty minutes to an hour when you will not be disturbed. You will need a journal, or a notepad and pen, music if it helps, and an open heart.

Allow yourself a visit to the moment you first felt the pain of a particular wound. Let your mind and memory concentrate, with the help of the following:

    ❀ As you go back in time to this painful moment, where specifically are you? A hospital, your childhood home, reading a letter not meant for you in your bedroom? Paint in the picture as fully as you can. Make use of sensory description: sight, smell, taste, and so forth. If it's a wound that has developed over time, visit several of the moments or incidents that were settings in which you felt (and feel) the pain.

❦ Who were you with when this wound was first inflicted? Did anyone else witness what occurred? If you were alone, did you want to be alone? Were you lonely?

If the wound took place in the distant past or your memory is a bit foggy, you may wish to use photographs, old letters, or possessions that will draw forth the scene and illuminate the wound more clearly. Don't be impatient if it doesn't all come at once. Allow it to unfold.

> *Whatever you can do or dream you can, begin it. Boldness has genius, magic and power in it. Begin it now.*
>
> ❧
>
> —*Goethe*

As the wound comes into focus, call it by its name. This may feel silly at first, but, in taking *Step One*, the naming process is crucial. When you have spoken the name of your wound or wounds, record in your journal the emotions or feelings that naming the wound brings forth: do you feel the stirrings of anger? Do you get a sense of fearfulness? Do you become anxious? Is there a heavy sadness that naming this wound engenders? Whatever the feeling or feelings, write each one down and comment on it freely.

The wound has its place and affects us. It is part of who we are today. In putting this into words, we are acknowledging that truth and taking the *First Step* on our journey toward being all we want to be.

THE RITUAL

On an evening when the stars are out, take fifteen minutes just to gaze at them, following these simple prompts:

❦ Pick one particular star. Concentrate on it. Notice its brightness and its position in the sky. It also has beauty. Now give that star the name of your wound.

❀ Next, pull your gaze back to take in the breadth of stars across the canvas of the sky.

❀ Our wound is a part of our lives in the same way that star is part of the sky. It has its place—its position in our firmament.

❀ Sit silently in the simple ritual of an acknowledgment of your wound.

❀ Bless the moment in which you viewed that star and saw clearly that wound.

If you live in a large metropolitan area where light grids make stargazing difficult, the same ritual can be accomplished with a painting. Concentrate on one part, a single aspect, of the painting—a color, a brushstroke, an object. That detail of the painting is your wound. Now draw your focus back, begin slowly to take in the complete picture, recognize that detail as one aspect of the complete whole—it is essential to the whole, but it does not dominate or overwhelm the whole.

Our lives are a work of art in that same way, wounds and all.

THE GIFT

The *miracles of self-knowledge* that emerge from acknowledging our wounds are part of the gift we have received by taking *Step One:*

❀ Awareness of my Sacred Wounds leads to a fuller, more complete awareness of myself.

❀ Being open to their message and learning from them means my wounds can be accessed or used to serve my personal growth.

❀ I am the only one who can put that growth to good use by sharing it with the people I come in contact with, by changing the way I treat them, the way I listen, the way I love.

✤ I can touch other lives by acknowledging the wounds in those with whom I interact, by speaking the truth to myself and to others.

—

In words written by Marianne Williamson and quoted by Nelson Mandela in his inaugural address: "As we are liberated from our own fear, our presence automatically liberates others." Such liberation is a continuing process, and we will make that recognition and awareness part of *Step Two*.

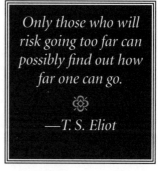

Only those who will risk going too far can possibly find out how far one can go.

—T. S. Eliot

The beauty of taking a *First Step* is that it leads you to the second. And you move ever forward. I like that direction.

How about you?

STEP TWO

LETTING GO OF GUILT: Entering the Kingdom of Healing

> *Guilt—the gift that keeps on giving.*
> —Erma Bombeck

THE MEDITATION

As I open to the healing waters of growth
Let those arrows sent forth from the bow of guilt
Turn away from my heart.
May the inner tension of blame be released
And roadblocks to my path to consciousness
Removed.

Strengthen my purpose.
Let me be open to the courage needed
To release the negative,
The harmful,
The ties I place around myself.
Forces that impede my progress.
May my spirit be freed within me
And may this journey be filled with
Small steps of wonder and discovery.

———

One of the most challenging inner impediments to claiming our Sacred Wounds is the very real need we often have to *place blame*. There are times when we take this blame game to the extreme—accusing everyone in our path of having a hand in the pain we've experienced. We turn against family, friends, at times even strangers. Somebody's got to be our scapegoat.

Of course, there usually *is* an individual or group that plays a part in inflicting our wounds or is fully responsible for them, and there is much to be gained in recognizing and accepting that someone has abused us or inflicted pain upon us. Clearly, identifying those who have contributed to our particular wound is part of the path to clarity that will enable us to make healthier choices for ourselves in the future. It is essential to moving on.

But there is, of course, another direction in which we send forth our *arrows of blame*. We aim them at ourselves. And with a direct hit on the target of our psyche and soul, a stream of guilt often springs forth within us. This attack upon our own person may take place on a subconscious level. On the other hand, some of us have been known to take ourselves on publicly, right there in the open, turning the spectacle of devouring our pride and dignity into a masochistic smorgasbord.

I remember one particularly uncomfortable experience. At a wedding I was attending, the best man got up to make the traditional toast. It started well enough, but before we all knew what had hit us the young man had lapsed into an animated, self-mocking speech about why he would never find true love. He insisted that, unlike his newly married friend, he possessed neither the looks nor the personality to deserve a wife. He was, he added with contempt that his forced laughter could not hide, a professional loser. The horrified groom, pretending it was a joke, relieved him of the microphone as the rest of the wedding guests looked on in stunned silence.

When we blame ourselves for wounds we have suffered due to unwise choices or the acts of others for which we take responsibility, we allow the pain to burrow inward, this, in turn, can cripple our ability to see our sorrow as an opportunity to enter the kingdom of healing.

This is not to say that we ought not take responsibility for causing hardship to ourselves or others. We are *the artists of our own lives* and have far more control over their composition than we often care to admit. And there are going to be times when, as artists, we are less than circumspect about the way we treat our own human canvas. Every painting will not be a masterpiece. Nevertheless, any artist who wallows in self-blame for errant brushstrokes on a particular painting not only harms herself, but mars in advance the canvas she could be creating.

Oscar Wilde had this to say about self-recrimination: "To regret one's own experiences is to arrest one's own development. To deny one's own experiences is to put a lie into the lips of one's life. It is no less than a denial of the soul." Guilt and self-blame are the living embodiments of regret. They hold our wounds hostage and lock

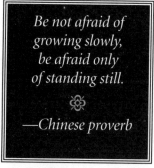

Be not afraid of growing slowly, be afraid only of standing still.

—Chinese proverb

them in one place, blocking our healing process. In their negative influence over how we view ourselves and the world around us, they deny the positive ability that sorrow and pain have to teach and enlighten us.

Guilt is anger, hurt, and frustration directed at ourselves. This is not just dangerous to the process of healing that can render our wounds *sacred*, but it may, in fact, threaten our lives and well-being. A 1996 report in the *Journal of Child Sexual Abuse* states that in a clinical sample of women who were sexually abused as children, those who were found to be *high self-blamers* proved to be more depressed and prone to self-mutilation and demonstrated weaker survival and coping skills than those with low self-blame tendencies. The idea that some of us actually work at holding on to such a debilitating attitude ought to be unnerving for anyone who wants to succeed.

THE BLAME GAME

*L*earning to let go of self-blame and the cycle of guilt is an essential step in recognizing our wounds as *sacred* and using them to transform our future. The guilt that grows out of blaming ourselves powers the voice that says we're not *good* enough, that we're only going to mess things up, that we'll never succeed. After all, we already blame ourselves for previous pain, and there's nothing to convince us that we've changed. Rather than being our own best destiny, we see ourselves as our own worst enemy. There's simply no room in our lives for the illumination of Sacred Wounds when our pain is being perpetuated by the darkness created by profane ones.

The first part of *Step Two* is to recognize that the blame game has a cyclical and destructive effect:

⚜ Some of us carry a burden of guilt around for never having told someone that we loved him or her before they died. We may even believe that we have contributed to an illness or death by this failure to communicate our affection. The wound of self-blame that results takes up a comfortable residence in our psyches and begins festering. Such a wound may manifest itself in a variety of self-destructive ways. We might, for example, avoid intimacy because, in our guilt, we believe we are destined to harm and sadden those we love.

⚜ Some of us may continue to make poor choices in love due to the misguided notion that we don't deserve the best. A woman who continues to enter abusive relationships because she doesn't believe she is entitled to being treated with dignity feels guilty for the suffering she's experienced, perhaps since childhood, and blames herself. When we find that our hearts have been abused, we often turn the finger of blame inward by reaffirming and setting in stone the belief that we are getting what we deserve. Our guilt produces a cycle of pain, so we mistreat ourselves again and again by making destructive choices in love. This ongoing circle in which we perpetuate our pain is what I call a *cycle wound*. It is hurt that plays itself out for as long as we're unwilling to let go of our falsely directed guilt and self-blame.

⚘ There are those of us who foster guilt because of our lack of success in our chosen field. Rather than believe that *every failure is an opportunity to try another path to our goal*, we interpret every setback as one more confirmation of our inherent incompetence. Period. But maybe success has been closed off to us because we continue to display and even broadcast our supposed imperfections. "Marinating" in this guilt may also be compounded by seeing and believing we are letting others down (parents, mate, children, friends). Before long, we become embittered and, in a self-fulfilling prophecy, continue along the path to failure.

These are but a few examples of how self-blame and the ensuing guilt injure us profoundly and keep us from growing into the people we truly want to be.

Sometimes the guilt and self-recrimination provide the foundation for a most passive life. We become bystanders in our own life as guilt closes down avenues of social and creative expression and, in the end, we become missing in action in the lives of those who love us and *need* us.

In other cases, the effects of guilt have a reverse effect. Instead

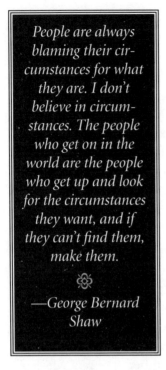

People are always blaming their circumstances for what they are. I don't believe in circumstances. The people who get on in the world are the people who get up and look for the circumstances they want, and if they can't find them, make them.

—George Bernard Shaw

of fostering passive, uncreative lives, our guilt manifests itself in an almost frenzied approach to living. We wield self-recrimination as if it were a scalpel, and we take that scalpel to our hearts and to our souls, puncturing the positive feelings that dare to begin their ascension within us. We're not "young enough," "pretty enough," "smart enough," we tell ourselves. The message that then seeps deep within the pores of our being is that we are, quite simply, *"Not enough, period."*

We may also turn outward, provoked by a guilt that has tethered itself to our spirit, and become petty and poisoned toward others: "Who's *he* to be dating a good-looking woman like that?" "Where does she get off asking for a raise—she's a nothing!" Worse, we may deliver stinging words and wounding insults to a child: "You never do anything right. Your whole life's going to be nothing, just like you." Yes, we can do a lot of damage with that instrument. We have that power.

THE POWER TO HEAL

If we agree that we have the power to hurt both ourselves and others, we must recognize conversely that we hold the power to heal. Speaking words that hurt or withholding words of love is a choice. Staying secluded and apart is a choice. Holding on to guilt over absent or abusive parents, the pain of a past medical crisis, sexual abuse, or having abused others is a choice. Viewing failure in work as an end rather than the means to success is a choice. Dragging around the past like a dead body on your back is a choice. We *choose* the life we lead. Yes, we are *that* powerful.

One element of *Step Two* is coming to see that healing is also a choice. In order to embrace it, we begin by asking ourselves some important questions:

- ❀ How can we see that guilt is a choice not an inevitability?
- ❀ How can we begin to let go of our self-blame and guilt, to recognize that we hold the key to its hold on us?
- ❀ How can we alter our journey in order to cross over from the no-man's-land of self-recrimination to the beckoning kingdom of healing?

We can answer these questions by choosing the pathway of forgiveness. Self-forgiveness. This act has the power not only to turn regret into rebirth, but it clears the road to discover our Sacred Wounds and the success they can give us. Just as we see and clearly feel the stark self-inflicted injuries of which we are capable, we are also able to envision the life-affirming tool of forgiveness within us, the healing waters of our own possibilities, should we so *choose*.

———

I want to share with you the story of someone who made such a journey. This is a young man who began his journey from the depths of despair, an endless pit that continued to be dug at the direction of his wounded spirit. He caught the violence he was doing to himself before it was too late, and out of his ability to *let go* of the guilt, fashioned a Sacred Wound that led to self-forgiveness, self-worth, and a presiding joy in life.

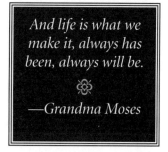

And life is what we make it, always has been, always will be.

—*Grandma Moses*

Brad's Story

*B*rad liked to eat. Really liked to eat. Like you and I breathe air. He and I were in the same junior high school, and we used to see each other at my father's family-style diner as we were growing up. One of the things I remember about Brad was the look on his face when he was downing a burger coupled with a double-double chocolate shake. My brother Mike told me that people only looked that way when they were having sex. What I didn't get then was how much trouble Brad was in and, despite that look of pleasure on his face when he inhaled his food, how very sad he was inside.

Brad and I shared a few classes at Edmunds Junior High. He had a giant-sized smile that seemed to go on forever. I thought then that this was both the biggest kid in school and the happiest. A group of us used to run over to grab lunch at the nearby YMCA. It sure beat the school cafeteria. I would occasionally catch sight of Brad carrying his lunch away from the snack shop counter. His order was always the same: two hot dogs, large fries, and a double order of chocolate milk. But because of his size, he became winded just walking to the Y, and it was becoming equally clear that Brad was in trouble. I began to hear taunts aimed his way: "Hey, fatboy, we got three seats over here with your name on them" and the equally cruel, "Hey, we don't need to build a float for the parade, let's just decorate Brad!"

But as is the way of fourteen-year-olds, none of us asked Brad what was going on in his life. I suppose it wasn't a "guy thing" to do, though it would have been a human thing to do. I lost contact with Brad as we continued through high school and college. In all my visits back home, his name never came up. I would have forgotten him completely were it not for a chance encounter on a visit to Vermont twenty-one years later.

Whenever I came back home, I went through a ritual that included a visit to the family restaurant, now run by my brother

Mike, a drive to Stowe for a visit to the Trapp Family Lodge (with a stop for homemade doughnuts and apple cider along the way), and a few laps around the track of my alma mater, the University of Vermont. It was during a run, on a gorgeous October day, that I found myself taking in the magnificent setting of blue sky, the Green Mountains in the distance, and the blazing gold and red glory of the changing leaves. As I made my final turn of the oval, I picked up the pace, sprinting to the end of my run. I was so focused on the natural setting surrounding me that I never noticed the starting blocks that studded the inner lanes at the end of the track. I must have simply run around them earlier, but suddenly I tripped and went down with a thud, rolling a few feet off the track and into the grass.

I was shaking off this rude surprise, and noticing an ugly scrape along my left leg, when a blurry figure appeared above me in the sunlight. "Hey, you all right? That was a bad one." The figure stretched out a hand to help me up. I took it, laughing at my own stupidity through the sting coming from my leg. When I was vertical, the man laughed in recognition, "Jan, my God, how are you?" I looked into the good-looking freckled face of a man about my age, sparkling blue eyes, rugged and healthy. "Don't you recognize me? It's me, Brad. We went to junior high together!"

It didn't compute. The man standing in front of me was trim, fit, and exuberant. Yes, something in the smile did look like Brad, but where was the rest of him?

Over the next couple of hours, in a halting stroll as I worked my leg out, and over coffee in the campus café, Brad and I caught up. His was an enthralling story of pain and redemption, and he shared it freely. The man in front of me had taken an astonishing journey in the secret shadow of his life, and his transformation fascinated me for its boldness and its affirmation. Because I was so captivated, or because, as he explained, he had taken my refraining from cruelty years earlier as a show of kindness (an appraisal I'm not sure I deserved), he blessed me with his story.

As a kid, Brad used to hear his parents fighting. What he experienced was not loud drunken brawls, but the escalating skir-
mishes that would start with a "drive-by" comment meant to
inflame. His mother and father traded insults as they passed in
the house, or when one of them was leaving for work. Brad
explained that he could predict when a verbal bullet was about to
be fired off by the way his parents would narrow their eyes and
stiffen their bodies. It got so that the young Brad could accurately
count down in seconds the time between the narrowing of the
eyes and the insulting remark. From there, angry words would fly
until their voices drowned out his cries of "Stop!" He told me that
he knew by the time he was eight that his parents probably never
should have married, and he began wishing they would divorce
so the terrible fighting would finally stop.

Brad began to store provisions in his room to cope with the
inevitable escalation of verbal assaults between his parents or the
terrible silence that seemed to echo even louder in the house.
Brad's stockpiling reminded me of the food supplies put aside in
the early sixties, when the threat of nuclear attack in America
spurred a national call for safety shelters in family basements
across the country. Brad was describing a battle plan in which his
safety shelter actually became a bedroom stocked with sweets,
chips, drinks, and sandwiches. Whenever he heard the fighting,
felt the loneliness of being caught in the middle, or experienced
the overwhelming sensation of being an *outsider* in his own
home, he turned to food for comfort. His eating became insa-
tiable because he was attempting to fill the yawning emptiness
inside him.

His parents divorced during his first year of high school. By
then, he had established a solid pattern of overeating to smother
the pain. But now, rather than feeling better that the fighting in
the house had stopped, Brad felt guilty for having wished for this
outcome. His mother was alone. His father seemed bitter whenever Brad would see him. His family had broken up, and it had

been one of his longtime, secret desires. He hated himself for the selfishness of his thoughts. Maybe they would eventually have worked things out. Maybe his eating had proven an embarrassment to them, which, in turn, had escalated the war of words. He was aware of the comments they both would make about his weight, and how they would blame each other for allowing their son to become fat and lazy. Brad said this all simply pushed him back to the plate, where he would gorge himself to assuage his bad feelings over having gorged himself in the first place.

When he moved out of his mother's house after high school, Brad's life was marked by utter passivity, devoid of joy or even the prospect of joy. He had a small apartment where he would spend a lot of time in the kitchen watching TV while cooking up pasta or roasting his favorite chicken dish. He'd push papers around from nine to five at the local assessor's office, where he filed field reports and downed giant cherry Slurpees. Late-night refrigerator raids, midnight pizza deliveries, and a strong craving for grinders washed down with chocolate milk marked his days. Before long he had become obese—over 320 pounds. His mother tried to get him to see a doctor. One of his colleagues at work even suggested that he join her at the local Weight Watchers, where they could help one another get in shape. But Brad couldn't see past the food or guilt in front of him. And the more others urged him to get help, the more he blamed himself for getting so heavy.

By the time he was twenty-three years old, Brad was resigned to this hopeless cycle of pain and powerlessness. He thought his mother had given up on him, too, but he didn't count on her resilience following her divorce and her abiding love for her only son.

Brad's mother had begun a new job in a local medical clinic. She had met someone, was dating, and seemed happier than she'd been in fifteen years. In her renewed passion for life, she turned her attention to Brad's problems. Brad told me, with some

awe, that he had never known his mother to have such perseverance, not to mention a great poker face. Under the pretext that
Brad's favorite uncle, also overweight, needed help, Brad's
mother convinced him that he was the only one who could persuade the uncle to go to the doctor. Brad's uncle, Ed, had always
been good to him; he took him to local sports games and introduced him to good food and music clubs when Brad's own parents were too miserable with each other to spend time with him.
Brad never forgot how much his uncle seemed to genuinely care
about him. The uncle *was* in danger, as of course was his nephew.
Although Brad couldn't find the path to helping himself, his
uncle's well-being was another matter.

So, with his mother's prodding, Brad insisted to his uncle that
by visiting the doctor, he could receive medicine for his high
blood pressure, which was essential to his survival. He accompanied Uncle Ed to the doctor's office only to find that it was Ed
who had been drafted by his mother to talk *Brad* into getting
help. Through a monumental effort of coaxing, tears, and physical restraint by his mother and uncle, Brad finally managed to get
into the doctor's examination room.

Brad was not surprised to hear he was in bad shape. What he
had not been prepared for was the doctor's prediction, announced
with utter conviction, that if Brad did not deal with his eating
problem and begin a diet and exercise regimen immediately, he
was going to *die an early death*. His heart would give out under
the physical duress of carrying so great a burden. Not *might* give
out; it was a certainty. Probably within ten years, the doctor told
him, twenty at the most.

Brad was shaken. His uncle and mother promised to provide
him with ongoing support. Brad tearfully agreed to start a program under the doctor's care. He then went home and gorged
himself on a pastrami grinder, a family-sized bag of chips, and a
pint of chocolate-chocolate chip ice cream. This was all *his fault.*
He was to blame for his condition and for making everyone

worry about him. He was intentionally ruining his life, and the only comfort he knew was to fill the hurt places with food. Despite his promises of just hours earlier, Brad was stuck in a cycle and couldn't see how to get out.

He might never have crawled out from under this medical warning and the ongoing guilt it engendered if it hadn't been for a traumatic and unexpected death. Not seven weeks after Uncle Ed had tried to help Brad in the doctor's office, he himself succumbed to a heart attack. At the age of forty-three, Uncle Ed was gone. The doctor attributed his death to high blood pressure, clogged arteries, a sedentary lifestyle, and a long history of overeating that had led to a final weight of 380 pounds.

Brad sank to his knees when he heard of the death of his uncle, and it was at his funeral that he made a promise to change. It was a pledge he would keep to the uncle he loved. He recognized that he was also making a promise to himself. There was some small place inside of him that acknowledged, in the face of his own ill health and the tragic loss of his uncle, that he was *worth* saving. It was an idea that seemed to spill out of him, as if he had tapped into a stream buried under years of sedimented guilt that had concealed a festering wound inflicted by years of parental fighting, and the loneliness of his own home. If he was going to keep this pledge, if he was going to rescue his life, he knew he would have to let go of this guilt.

Brad began a strict regimen under his physician's care. Slowly, he began to alter not just his eating habits but his whole way of life. He started a walking program at the local Y, where years earlier he had regularly downed those hot dogs and chocolate-milk lunches. He began reading, devouring some of the books he'd avoided in high school. Instead of a constant diet of television along with his pasta, Brad purposely chose the affirmations of Kahlil Gibran and became dazzled by the boyish pranks of Mark Twain's Huckleberry Finn.

Once he had lost enough weight, he joined a more aerobic

exercise class and received the support of colleagues at work who were inspired by his example. With the tiny successes that began to emerge as he shed pounds, Brad felt a growing self-esteem and confidence. He began to experience a new and vibrant *hopefulness*. It was a feeling he hadn't known before. And it tasted better to his soul than any of the food he had binged upon.

Yet there was a nagging part of this long road back to health that still had to be addressed. It occurred to Brad that the blame he had inflicted on himself, the guilt he had carried for so long, had worked its way into his very being. This pain had spurred his overeating and continued to feed his sense of hopelessness and loneliness over the years. He could not dismiss it so easily as an unwanted inhabitant of his life's past. Through counseling and a journal of discovery he was keeping, he began to understand that the wounds of his childhood were real and continued to speak to him. They would be part of his new life, whether or not he wished them there. He could either allow these wounds to continue to be attached to guilt, or he could liberate his wounds and learn from them. He could use them to remind himself of his right to make his own choices, choices that would govern his life, both negatively and positively.

In order to allow this healing to progress, to free these wounds to speak *to* him directly rather than *through* his sedimented guilt, Brad came to a realization that was as profound in its simplicity as it was difficult to accomplish: he needed to forgive himself. With all the things he now wanted out of life, there could be no future if he could not let go of the blame he had fed upon for so long.

Brad devised a ritual for himself. He would go for a walk along the edge of Lake Champlain, a spectacularly beautiful body of water across which one can see the shores of New York State. Holding some item of food, either leftovers from a meal or a slice of bread he brought along for the occasion, Brad would consciously itemize those things for which he blamed himself: his

parents' fighting, their divorce, his lack of self-discipline, allowing himself to become obese, choosing to comfort himself by
overeating, damaging his health, refusing help. With each mention of guilt, Brad would toss a piece of food upon the water (no
doubt a feast for the local fish and geese!). After letting go of the
guilt through this ritual, Brad would conclude the act with a simple benediction that he had come across and written in his journal: "*I have the power to forgive and to live. Make my choices
worthy of me. And let me be worthy of them.*" It spoke to him, and
became his mantra.

Each time Brad took part in this ritual or otherwise consciously separated out his self-denigration from his emotional
injuries, he was giving his wounded self a chance to teach him
and bless him with the power of choice. Through ongoing therapy and his self-inspired rituals and affirmations, Brad moved
into the rebirth of his life. And with his act of self-forgiveness, he
had begun to transform his wound from a negative trauma into a
positive teacher, from the *profane* to the *sacred.*

Brad continued on his path to redemption, healing through
acts of self-love and the positive reinforcement that comes from
growing into the lifetime of possibilities he had always wanted for
himself. Just two and a half years after his beloved uncle's death,
Brad had built a solid and affirming foundation for the future.
With the renewal of his life, and in finally seeing in himself someone worthy of happiness, Brad enrolled in college, majoring in
business management. As he continued to slim down and felt
more positive about who he was, he began to take a more active
part in social settings, even involving himself in the Junior
Olympics and student government. Oh, yes . . . and he began
dating.

Brad's metamorphosis had occurred nine years before I met
up with him again on the track at the university. With the widest
grin I'd ever seen, Brad pulled a photo from his wallet and, as we
stood midcampus on that autumn afternoon, he showed me the

picture of a lovely woman with a smile to match his own. She was holding a baby girl who had her fingers raised to her mother's face. This was his wife and their newborn daughter.

"I never thought I deserved any of this," he told me, shaking his head, still smiling. "I got the brass ring. And you know something?" Brad held my gaze with a profound expression of contentment: "We all deserve it. Every one of us."

He handed me his card as we said good-bye. I looked down to read the title under his name: *Director of Human Services*. Brad, who could never get out of his own way, was now overseeing the workforce of a local corporation. As I watched him getting into his car, he gave me an exuberant thumbs-up. I realized that Brad had kept his promise—to his uncle and to himself. And in sharing his story, he had shown me not only how powerful we each can be in changing the course of our lives, but that redemption comes with a smile as big as your dreams.

———

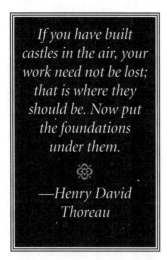

If you have built castles in the air, your work need not be lost; that is where they should be. Now put the foundations under them.

—Henry David Thoreau

Brad found his way to the life of his dreams only when he was prepared to release himself from the guilt that had encased him for years. In breaking through and letting go, he laid claim to a pain that no longer threatened his success. His wounds ultimately provided him with the energy he needed to act and taught him in a profound and life-altering way that he himself possessed the power to transform his own destiny.

We, like Brad, can see that self-blame comes at a heavy price. And we can see with ever more clarity that we do not wish to pay the exorbitant cost that guilt imposes on our emotional and physical well-being. We ask ourselves the question: *what percentage of our lives do we wish to spend on guilt and what percentage on success?* You and I both know the answer. Spending even a fraction of the precious time we are on this earth laying blame upon our own hearts is a waste of life's blessing. Giving up even a fragment of our potential to a cycle of pain over which we ultimately have control is a transgression against our very souls.

Norman Cousins called life "an adventure in forgiving." *Step Two*, Letting Go of Guilt, is an essential element of that adventure. Because rooting out why we blame ourselves, why we induce guilt, why we wound our own hearts, takes us to the entrance of the kingdom of healing. It is then that we can enter, but only when self-forgiveness gives us the key.

THE TASK

Now we must look within, become detectives of our own inner worlds, to investigate our pain and patterns. Blaming ourselves has not only produced guilt that has wounded our souls, it has curtailed our dreams, altered our decisions and choices, and confined us to a life of fear and self-recrimination. By tracking down the self-defeating cycles for which we alone are responsible and over which we alone have control, we can consciously interrupt and "arrest" them, replacing self-sabotage with choices that will guarantee our success.

Take yourself on a walk, head to a café, or lie on your bed, whatever allows you time alone to think. At this moment, take out your journal and respond to these questions. Be as specific as you possibly can. Having the courage to shine a light on the cost of your guilt and self-blame will allow you to take a giant step toward bankrupting the pain bank that you've been drawing on for years. Ask yourself:

❀ Has blaming yourself and holding on to guilt cost you in terms of *goals, ambitions, lifestyle,* and/or *happiness?*

❀ Has your guilt led you to settle for less out of life?

❀ Has your guilt undermined your choices of where you want to be in your career?

❀ Has it kept you from seeking, or believing you deserve, a mate or the *kind* of mate you deserve?

❀ Has the wound of guilt you've carried proven a danger to either your physical or mental health? Have you sabotaged yourself through addiction to alcohol, sex, work?

❀ Has allowing the growing sense of self-blame within you made you more cynical and less lovable to others? How about in your own eyes?

❀ Has this wound kept you from feeling hopeful, helpful, healthy, happy?

> *Twenty years from now you will be more disappointed by the things that you didn't do than by the ones you did do. So throw off the bowlines. Sail away from the safe harbor. Catch the trade winds in your sails. Explore. Dream. Discover.*
>
> ❀
>
> *—Mark Twain*

In recording the answers to these questions, you are focusing on self-defeating *cycle wounds* that keep you mired in a vicious circle of pain and self-punishment.

Weigh the cost of this life, and decide if you're willing to continue to bankroll it. If not, let us recognize that there is an alternative. We can let go of the guilt and stop nourishing our pain and powerlessness.

By taking *Step Two,* we begin to forgive ourselves for acts we may have committed and for which we have long ago paid our dues. We can see that we are worth a better life than this, a healthier one, and we can determine that the time has come to lay claim to it.

THE RITUAL

Brad created a ritual that almost exactly duplicates one I take part in once a year. Jews at the High Holy Days perform the ceremony of *Tashlikh*—casting transgressions symbolically on the water, using bread crumbs to signify the crumbs of negativity that the individual is letting go.

⊛ If you live near a body of water—the ocean, a lake, a stream or river—by all means avail yourself of its peaceful and life-giving company. If it isn't practical, not to worry. You can create a serene bath in your own home. You may wish to light some candles and immerse yourself in the tub . . . just you and the water.

⊛ Standing by the water or immersed in the bath, concentrate on the guilt you have felt, the blame you have carried, and the pattern of self-defeating actions, the *cycle wounds,* that this pain has engendered. Identify the wound and specifically what led or what leads you to self-recrimination. *(I get in trouble when I try to communicate, so I eat, watch TV, and stay away from people; I got hit because I said things that bothered my father—it's my fault; I never told my mother I loved her, she died after one of our fights, I don't deserve love.)*

⊛ Taking the bread crumbs—or bath beads, if at home— toss them into the water, consciously letting go of the guilt you have carried. Name that for which you have blamed yourself, and free its hold on your heart. With purpose and forgiveness, remove its grip on you. With courage, toss this guilt into the water and allow it to be carried away from your life or be dissolved. As you do, you may want to speak the words with which Brad blessed his own ritual: "*I have the power to forgive and to live. Make my choices worthy of me. And let me be worthy of them.*"

You may choose to compose your own prayer of forgiveness, or find other words that speak to your unique sensibility or situation. The important thing here is the act, the ritual, whereby humans bless a moment in their lives and bestow meaning. It is not the crumbs or the water or the words that carry significance. It is our involvement, infusing ourselves into the symbolic act, that makes it sacred. For we, ourselves, are sacred.

THE GIFT

In the *miracles of self-knowledge* we celebrate taking *Step Two,* in which we let go of the guilt to claim the healing that is within our Sacred Wounds. These affirmations serve as cornerstones of the new foundation we are building, and they will help us to see our wounds, not as the enemy, but as the fertile soil in which we can renew our emotional and spiritual roots:

- ❀ Letting go of the guilt, the blame I've placed on myself, liberates me to move more freely in the direction of my own success.
- ❀ The price of negative-producing guilt is too costly for the life I want to lead. I will not pay it.
- ❀ I alone can forgive myself for the harm I've caused through self-recrimination. I deserve that gift of love.
- ❀ My wounds can bless me with healing through the lesson they teach that we are powerful enough to both hurt and help ourselves.
- ❀ By letting go of the burden of guilt I have shouldered, I am free to grow, to hope, and to dream.

In taking this *Second Step*, "Letting Go of Guilt," we acknowledge that it is only in letting go of what keeps us moored to self-blame that we can enter the realm of healing—a kingdom that exists within us and to which we hold the key not *despite* but *because* of our Sacred Wounds.

Now we are prepared to embark on *Step Three*, where we will learn to drain away the *profane* elements that reside in our wounds in order to uncover the *sacred* that awaits us.

STEP THREE

DRAINING THE PROFANE FROM THE PAIN: In Search of
the Sacred

> *What wound did ever heal but by degrees?*
> —William Shakespeare

THE MEDITATION

Allow me the gift of discernment
To separate out the messages that confound my life,
To drain away the cold unceasing cacophony of pain
That drowns the sacred song that seeks my soul.

In the quiet of my healing
May I uncover the art of listening.
And let me be clear of eye
To differentiate the gold within my life's wounds
From that alloy that lessens my worth.

That I may draw closer to the fullness of my spirit.
That I might occupy the hallowed ground
of my own growth.

———

The Maori have a proverb: "Turn your face to the sun and the shadows fall behind you." It is our task now to put the shadows, the *profane,* behind us, and face the glistening light, the *sacred,* waiting in our wounded spirits. By doing so, we are traveling beyond *Steps One* and *Two,* in which we both acknowledged our wounds and let go of the guilt that denied us the journey toward claiming our Sacred Wounds.

In *Step Three,* we seek out those elements of our wounds that keep us unaware of our own power and purpose, and that sacred element of our pain that can elevate us to consciousness and change. Here we will differentiate between the shadow world, marked by untruths and false assumptions, and the real world, a state of awareness of our true potential. In truth, by claiming responsibility for our journey in this manner, by becoming *conscious* of it, we are contributing to the universe. How? By healing and transforming our small corner of it, we heal a part of the world. In repairing ourselves, we help to repair the world.

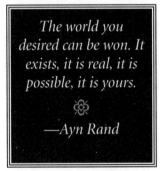

The world you desired can be won. It exists, it is real, it is possible, it is yours.

—Ayn Rand

Mircea Eliade, a renowned authority on myths and religion, insists that the *sacred* in life "is a structure of human consciousness." I interpret this as saying that we are all capable of realizing and creating the *sacred* in life—only by way of consciousness. Consciousness is a state of awareness of who, what, and where we are. When we operate in this reality we see things as they are, not as we might want them to be. We recognize the truth about ourselves and our circumstances and reject life in the mired world of half-truths and self-deception. In such a reality, we are capable of seeing the *sacred,* even bringing it into being. The *sacred* is that which calls us to our higher purpose in life and elevates how we see ourselves and others. It instills in us passion for our approach to life and unveils the inner power with which we can create success. The *sacred* is the inspiration and light that give our life meaning by appealing to the best within us while making us aware of the potentially destructive aspects that reside within us as well. When our wounds provide that light, that meaning, and that direction, then they are, indeed, *Sacred Wounds.*

Conversely, what removes us from finding such meaning, what steers us into living inauthentic and nonproductive lives, can be referred to as *profane.* The pain and wounds that pull us away from who we want to be, that plunge us into the darkness of insecurity and fear, that lead us into lives of falseness through deception and denial—these are *profane wounds.* They prevent us from coming to know the reality of *who we were meant to be.* They misdirect us by giving out messages of hopelessness, which, in turn, foster apathy. They diminish the path we want for ourselves, shrinking it into a tiny bridge across a vast canyon that makes success look terrifying, if not impossible. They can also convince us that we can drown our pain with vodka, cocaine, anger, detachment, guilt. By settling for less in our life, we are threatening our well-being and happiness.

"THERE'S MORE TO THE SURFACE THAN MEETS THE EYE"

*D*r. Aaron Beck is one of the founders and leaders of the Cognitive Therapy movement, which is a well-defined branch of psychotherapy treating a wide range of psychological problems, including depression, anxiety, anger, marital conflict, loneliness, panic, fear, eating disorders, substance abuse, and personality problems. The focus of CT is on the way we think, behave, and communicate in the here and now, rather than on our early childhood experiences (which is the focus of psychoanalysis). Beck has shown that our thought processes can literally *produce* events that happen to us which, in turn, radically affect our thinking and expectations. In other words, *what we believe* is largely determined by our *experience*. Moreover, what we think and believe help to determine how we view the world around us and, perhaps most important, ourselves. For example, the devastating loss of a long-term relationship that was headed for marriage, followed by dating that ends in rejection, may cause the wounded person to avoid intimacy on the grounds that he or she is undesirable. A child who's been neglected or abused may view the world as something to fear and therefore grows up to act with timidity, like a bud holding itself tight, afraid to blossom. In both cases, experience and identity merge into pain that poisons growth.

Based on Beck's forty years of clinical research, the key to many of our psychological difficulties, then, is not deep in our unconscious, but in patterns we have established over long periods of time (sometimes a lifetime). This dysfunctional thinking, rather than being a product of the unconscious, is much closer to *conscious awareness*. As Beck likes to put it: "There is more to the surface than meets the eye."

For twenty years I have served as an educator/administrator in a private day school, and have had the opportunity to teach many young people. Adolescence is a trying time, as we all know. As youngsters move through this stage, they are getting their bearings as to who they are and where they fit in. Countless times, I have witnessed teenagers who had unexplainably poor images of themselves. They might have been attractive young men or women with clear intellects, who were delightful to know through written assignments or one-on-one exchanges. But in a larger setting, these individuals often donned a false self, their self-confidence seeming to dissolve as they hid behind an image or facade (as was noted in the Introduction in speaking of "masking" our wounds). This often evidenced itself in timid or unconfident behavior, a *conscious awareness* of a perceived worthlessness.

I knew one young man who seemed to me possessed of

unusual insight and a poetic soul. Yet in public he kept to the shadows, rarely talking to others, never speaking up unless he was addressed directly. He began going out at night to "tag" public property, painting his name in wild colors on underpasses and store walls, a cry to the universe that he existed. When the police picked him up, his parents were stunned. He was usually so quiet in his room that they never even knew he was missing!

> *Healing may not be so much about getting better as about letting go of everything that isn't you— all the expectations, all the beliefs—and becoming who you are.*
>
> ❀
>
> *—Rachel Naomi Remen*

I could see both the inner and outer beauty of such individuals, but my view of their obvious merits often contrasted dramatically with the "false truth" under which they operated. It's not unusual for shy teens to look in the mirror and see untold faults. They feel they cannot venture an opinion in public because "who'd want to listen to me?" These teens' belief systems are based on the dysfunctional and false thinking that they are clumsy and woefully unattractive. This is their "truth," and it undermines their approach to living. It will remain their "truth" as long as their *core beliefs* remain the same.

Many adults also see themselves through the same mistaken lenses. We conduct an inner self-deprecating monologue in which we constantly berate ourselves that we are unattractive, uninteresting, without worth. This is a *core belief,* a belief that we hold to be true about ourselves at the very center of our being, and it is based in the pain we've experienced from our wounds. This pain has distorted our self-image and our view of the world with a *profane* lens. We are mired in the ugliness and poison of our injured souls, unable to hear or see the *sacred* elements in those very same wounds or in the world around us. Thus we often find ourselves living our lives in *self-defeating* ways. We may even foster the *cycle wounds* referred to in *Step Two*, injuring ourselves again and again. Individuals who approach life with the core beliefs that they are inferior, unattractive, or worthless often act in dysfunctional ways, and often through promiscuity, physical aggression, or other negative, self-destructive behaviors.

Our challenge in *Step Three* will be to recognize within ourselves these wounds of self-defeat and to identify the dysfunctional emotional maps that direct us away from our best interests. Our journey to who we want to be, even who we were meant to be, is not going to be helped by accepting a life with these *profane* impulses sabotaging our success. Stepping out of the shadow of our core beliefs and draining away that which poisons the *sacred* message that we can become more, not less, is essential to our personal growth. We don't have to settle for living in pain. Our quest is to claim the illumination and empowering energy of our Sacred Wounds that lead us to a life of meaning, happiness, and success.

DRAINING THE POISON WITH ALTERNATIVE BELIEFS

*A*nother pioneer in the field of Cognitive Therapy, Dr. Albert Ellis, has fashioned a variation on dealing with core beliefs that can do a great deal to remove the shadows of dysfunctional thinking. His approach is called Rational Emotive Behavioral Therapy (REBT). Like Dr. Beck, he believes that our irrational beliefs about ourselves lead to long-term, disabling life problems. For example, a depressed person feels sad and lonely because he erroneously thinks he is inadequate and a failure. A therapist using REBT would show the depressed person his or her successes and challenge the belief that he or she is inadequate, rather than attacking the depression itself.

Ellis argues that we become conditioned to "thinking errors which lead us to make absolute statements to ourselves," declarations that box us in to a debilitating core belief. Statements such as "If I'm not outstandingly competent, I am completely worthless." "Others should always treat me considerately, or they are absolutely rotten." "The world must always give me happiness, or I will die." Holding fast to such either/or thinking, Ellis would point out, causes us to *ignore the positive, exaggerate the negative*, and "overgeneralize." These erroneous thoughts and their negative influence on our ability to grow are what I mean when I refer to the *profane* that emanates from our wounds.

Let us examine a specific wound to see more clearly what is meant by a *core belief* and how that belief alters the "truth" under which we operate. The wound we will use here is one we will all have to go through at some point in our lives, if we haven't already—the loss of a loved one. As a result of this particular wound we might create a core belief—"I am all alone in the world. No one cares about me." A therapist following this approach would ask, How does this belief make us feel? We might respond, "It makes me feel sad, deserted, depressed, alone." And that would be the truth, our truth, for we are indeed sad and lonely. No argument there. But following REBT, the therapist would now use his or her skills to argue against these ideas, or, even better, lead the client to make his own contrary arguments. For example, a therapist using this approach would ask us to search our hearts and our recent experiences for evidence that this core belief is not the whole truth. We might find ourselves saying, "Maybe I am not *always* alone—my kids call me; people do reach out to me, even the grocer is always friendly." We might even concede, "My capacity for joy hasn't been destroyed completely. Even though I am sad, sometimes I still take pleasure from simple things like Monet's paintings, a beautiful garden, music that may bring up memories but is bittersweet."

We might then be asked in therapy to consider an *alternative belief* based on this new evidence. We then could convincingly reason: if my "truth" isn't actually based on the facts of my life, if there is proof that I am *not* alone, that I *am* capable of happiness, that people *do* care, perhaps that alternative view might replace my core belief? Of course, pain and suffering can also be our "truth" at times in our lives, and they can be very real. But remember, the goal here is to drain away the *false* message, the *profane*, that emanates from our wounds, and turn to the true messages, the *sacred*, that also exist in the wounds. In coming to see a more complete and undistorted picture of the "truth," we receive a *sacred* communication—*pain need not be a way of life*, and *an attitude of affirmation can truly be our companion.*

By linking our wounds to an alternative belief, to a new and *empowering* core belief, we come to realize that the wound has not stopped us—that we can *go on.* That is a liberating and heal- ing thought, one that dysfunctional, false beliefs could never fos- ter. We begin to see the canvas of our lives more truly and, as with the ritual in *Step One*, we find our wound is an integral part of the whole wonder of who we are.

Our ability to *value* our experience—our pain—at a deeper level brings us into contact with the *sacred* part of the wound. And with that contact, something even more valuable happens— we begin to *make meaning.* A simple and profound truth I have discovered through my own pain, and one that I've shared when counseling others, is essentially this:

> **We may not be able to choose our wounds in life,**
> **but we do have the power to choose**
> **what those wounds are going to mean.**

———

For me, experiencing "grace" is something that happens when I hold my wife at sunset, witness my baby daughter's latest dis- covery, listen to a moving symphony, or become transfixed by a moment of truth in the theater. But there are also human beings who embody this quality of grace. They are "living grace," and they transform us by simply touching us in our hearts. Somehow they bring out the *sacred* in us. One such person is Lena. And in her story you will find the purging of what is *profane* in her pain and the revelation that *one's wounds can bestow a higher consciousness.*

That is a core belief that will always serve the best within us—even at the most challenging of times.

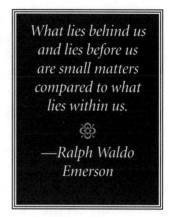

What lies behind us and lies before us are small matters compared to what lies within us.

—Ralph Waldo Emerson

Lena's Story

A few years ago, I came into the office on a bright summer morning to find a message on my voice mail. I heard a woman's voice. I couldn't make out the accent, and she didn't identify herself in any way. The message simply said that there was a young woman who needed to speak with me. I would find her at a local hospital, the name of which the voice supplied. The patient's name was Lena, and she had ovarian cancer. The last thing the anonymous voice said was that "it would mean a great deal if you could find it in your heart to pay her a visit . . ." A pause and then the voice added, "Today." And with that there was a *beep,* and the mysterious caller was gone. Had the caller forgotten to leave her name or had she meant to be mysterious? Was she a relative, a friend, a physician? And why would this young woman, whose name I didn't recognize, want to speak with me? I hadn't even finished my first cup of coffee, and already the day had unfolded like a giant question mark.

Later that afternoon, I stole away from a faculty meeting, pulled up to the hospital, and found myself in the oncology unit. Having stopped first at the nurses' station, I was told that no one had any idea who might have phoned me. I was informed that the patient had a father and a brother who visited often. And there were a few friends. Perhaps one of them had called? At any rate, as one nurse noted, I was there, and Lena would appreciate the visit. I nodded, turned, and walked down the corridor to her room. The door was closed. I knocked and a soft voice, barely audible, invited me in.

There, resting in her bed, I found Lena. I was instantly struck by how young she looked. Her face was smooth and almost child-like. Her eyes shone bright yet with a calming softness (I would find out later that she was twenty-nine years old). Bald from chemo treatments and dressed in a white flannel nightgown, Lena sat up against a wall of pillows and smiled. Alert and gracious, she asked me to sit. I stammered an introduction and told her about the phone call. She told me that she'd never heard of me, nor did she know any woman with an accent. Nevertheless, she seemed genuinely pleased that I was there, and very eager to ask me something. I sat, forgetting about the perplexing identity of the mystery caller, and taking in a woman who seemed to beam with serenity. When I introduced myself and told her I was a rabbi, she asked if it was all right to call me by my first name. "I prefer that," I told her. "Then Jan," she began, "let me ask you a favor." I nodded. Then she made a simple and profound request: "Tell me about God."

I didn't know what to say. And, realizing that I didn't know what to say, it immediately occurred to me that someone who's been ordained in any religion ought to have a ready answer to such a request. *Tell me about God?* Good Lord, that's like a major-league batter being served up a nice, slow, underhand pitch right across the plate. Home-run time.

Lena studied my face, my silence. And I heard myself say, "Can you believe it, in all my years in the rabbinate, that is the first time anyone's put that question to me?" I could see in her eyes how much she wanted an answer, and I struggled against the impulse to fall back on any canned religious platitudes.

In the silence that had been created, I also noticed the calm that existed in the room. It was certainly not coming from me. And, just like that, I knew what to say: "Actually, Lena, why don't you tell *me*?"

Now it seemed as though I were the one who'd pitched the nice, easy lob across the plate, for, as it became clear immediately, Lena had been waiting for just that question. She wanted to tell me; she *needed* to tell me. She had knowledge of the *profane* experience of her cancer, which had drawn her from her previously normal everyday life into the pain and disorientation of hospitals and IV drips and calculated timetables of life expectancy. But there was also something clearly wondrous that was about to be unveiled. Lena shimmered with a positive and profound energy. She'd uncovered something *sacred* in her suffering and, with a small but luminescent voice, she proceeded to tell me about God. Slowly, and with great passion, Lena revealed to me the power of how her physical and spiritual wounds had elevated her life.

Lena had always been a full-energy person; she had played sports in high school and danced as if her life depended on it at parties in college. Traveling after graduation, she'd spent time in England, Spain, Holland, and Italy. The latter was her favorite. She adored Tuscany, and even took a class on the art of the Renaissance while there. In her early twenties, she came back to the States and kicked around, looking for a niche. She found it, of all places, on a beach in Malibu.

One day, while sprawled out comfortably on her blanket on the sand, she noticed a group of women at a set of easels set in the sand nearby. Wandering over, she saw that they were each busy rendering an interpretation of the scene before them. One was concentrating on capturing the crash of the waves; another took a strolling older couple as her focus. Before she knew it, Lena was deep in conversation with the facilitator of this painting class, who told her that it was part of a local art complex that fostered personal expression among seniors. The same facility also offered art expression, dance, and poetry classes for children after school and on weekends. Intrigued, Lena visited the center the following Saturday and, before she knew it, had been offered a job helping to coordinate classes and schedules. She loved it. The energy was amazing, she told me, her face ablaze. At the time she was twenty-three, and it seemed like a good place to be. She had her whole life ahead of her. She could always move on.

Five years later, Lena was still working at the art complex, teaching a class in movement to elderly women and weekend dance classes to children. Although she wasn't an accomplished dancer, she knew enough to get kids on the floor and encourage them to express their creativity. She had been dating someone she had met a year earlier, and was planning to return to the university for graduate work in performance art. But one afternoon she noticed that she was feeling a little bit off. She felt more tired than usual, and it seemed as though she was always full, although her eating habits hadn't changed. If anything, she sometimes felt waves of nausea that would certainly have prevented her overeating.

Her first thought was that she was pregnant, even though she and her boyfriend had used birth control very carefully. But now that she thought about it, sex hadn't been too great for a while, because she was feeling some pain during intercourse. And there *was* a suspicious swelling in her abdomen. Lena made straight for her obstetrician/gynecologist. To her relief, she wasn't pregnant. But why was she always tired? Why was her pelvic area so sensitive and distended? And why did it hurt to make love?

Over the next few months, Lena told me, she was diagnosed with a variety of ailments: irritable bowel syndrome, endometriosis, and extreme stress. She went from doctor to doctor, searching for answers and for someone who actually knew what to do when they were found. During this difficult period, her relationship broke up. Due to her increasing discomfort and exhaustion, friends had to cover her classes at work. One physician suggested that the problem was probably psychosomatic.

Perhaps, he suggested, she had a fear of intimacy. Such was the medical maze she endured. With her fifth doctor's visit, however, the maze-wandering ended, with a diagnosis that hit her over both head and heart. Lena had ovarian cancer.

As Lena soon learned, ovarian cancer is referred to as "the disease that whispers," because the symptoms, particularly early on, are not intense enough for most women to notice. As she looked back, she realized that she'd been suffering from mild fatigue for months, maybe even a couple of years. She had responded by taking more vitamins and increasing her exercise regimen. She had been urinating more frequently for a while, but had simply chalked that up to her water intake. Now she was told that these were all warning signs of ovarian cancer, which she learned, with considerable alarm, ranked fifth in overall cancer deaths among women.

While still reeling from this news, Lena was immediately scheduled for surgery. Her father, brother, and friends gathered at the hospital to lend support. Her mother had died some years earlier, a victim of breast cancer. That's why Lena had been so careful to have mammograms each year from her mid-twenties on. But as she would later find out, there was no test for ovarian cancer. Besides, she wouldn't have thought to have one even if there were. It simply wasn't on her radar screen—or on the screens of any of the physicians she had already seen.

The news got worse. Surgery revealed that Lena wasn't in the earliest stages of this disease. There are fours stages of cancer. Stage 1 is the most treatable, Stage 4 the least. Lena had Stage 4 ovarian cancer. It had advanced beyond the region of her ovaries, and was detected as far away as the fluid surrounding her lungs. She was told that in 1996 the survival rate beyond five years stood at 15 to 20 percent (as opposed to the five-year survival rate of Stage 1 ovarian cancer, which was 90 percent).

During surgery Lena's doctors removed her ovaries, but her gynecologic oncologist explained that that was only a first step.

They would also have to deal with the metastatic cancer cells that had spread. It was at this point that Lena began her spiritual and emotional journey, confronting God in anger, and discovering hidden resources within herself she had never known existed.

As she related her story to me during a series of several visits, Lena never flinched from recalling the ugly facts about her initial response. Rather than retreating into her fear after her prognosis, she had burst into a frenzy of activity, as if she might work the cancer within her to death. Her father, a local businessman, urged her to get counseling and allow herself the freedom to take it easy. He gave her money and made calls to psychologists, cancer specialists, anyone who might be able to help. But Lena didn't want to take it easy. In fact, as soon as she recovered from surgery, she immersed herself in schedules and in teaching dance classes. The whole thing was unfair, and she was the only one she could count on, so to hell with the specialists! She wasn't going to listen to anyone because the truth was, as far as she was concerned, nobody gave a damn. Not really. Their lives would go on as usual, unlike hers. Besides, maybe it would all just go away. Keeping busy effectively kept all that was happening to her at arm's length.

The week before she was supposed to begin chemotherapy, it all caught up with her. She had taught her class of young girls that day with a particular fervor; she was alive with movement and energy. Lena had reveled in the excited responses of the girls dancing around her, feeding off their enthusiasm and sending it back out through her feet. After the girls had left, Lena paused to catch her breath, leaning against the wall and holding her pelvis, where three weeks earlier her ovaries had been. It was tender, and she had no business trying to dance. But she was doing it anyway.

And then she heard the small voice of one of her students behind her. Lena turned to see a nine-year-old cherub beaming from ear to ear. "Thanks, Lena," she said. "Today was my best day.

I really felt like a dancer, you know. And it's all 'cause of you." She came up and put her arms around Lena's waist, hugging tightly. Lena watched as if outside herself, hugging the little girl back, awed and thankful for the human contact. And then the girl was gone, and Lena was left in the studio alone. She sank to her knees, a sob growing from deep within her. She held her abdomen, and her tears poured down with ferocity. She was never going to have a little girl. She would never have children. The cancer had robbed her of that. It wasn't the thought of dying that was so overpowering, she suddenly realized. It was the denial of her potential to bear life.

Over the next week, she spent her days and nights in anger. And the anger turned to hatred. What kind of a God does this to good people? Who had she ever hurt to deserve this? She lashed out at her brother when he came by for a visit, telling him it wasn't fair that he had never been sick a day in his life. She'd always been the one looking out for him when they were growing up. Why hadn't God spread the suffering around? She caused her best friend to dissolve into tears when demanding that the woman stop being so selfish by spending time with her fiancé when Lena was so ill. And when her father brought dinner by on the night before the first chemo treatment, Lena tore into him for not warning her after her mother's death that children with a family history of breast cancer are at increased risk for ovarian cancer. He'd never known that, he said. But Lena wasn't listening to any excuses. When he told her that he'd been praying for her every day, it was the last straw. Screaming that God hadn't done anything to help her mother, that God was nothing but a worthless bastard who hated her as much as she hated Him, Lena picked up a treasured dish that had once been used for her mom's special desserts and smashed it on the floor in front of her astonished father. After a moment he went to Lena, enfolded her in his arms, and the two wept together into the night.

The next day, during her chemo treatment, Lena sat helplessly while powerful drugs pumped into her, hoping against hope that they could destroy all vestiges of the cancer cells coursing through her body. Fighting with everyone who loved her wasn't going to make her feel better. They weren't the enemy; the cancer was. She knew that, but there was a darkness growing within her, and all she wanted now was light. It was then that Lena chose to drop her mask of anger, and the frenzied distance from others that she had worked so hard to construct, and ask for help. She didn't know where or to whom exactly her request was directed. She only knew that her life was threatened, and she wasn't going to roll over. Nor was she going to work herself into the ground as a way of ignoring the presence of her wound.

While experiencing the nausea, loss of appetite, headaches, and hair loss that come with chemotherapy, Lena began to search for a counterbalance to her suffering. The actual pain and sense of bereavement were immense. Lena came to a conclusion based on a principle of art she had learned years earlier in Tuscany. Artists often use contrasting colors to underscore their work, sometimes changing brushstrokes for added measure. In order to survive, she realized, she would need to use contrasts in her own life—brushstrokes of optimism and creativity to counter the destruction going on in her body and, perhaps more important, in her soul.

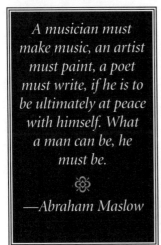

A musician must make music, an artist must paint, a poet must write, if he is to be ultimately at peace with himself. What a man can be, he must be.

—*Abraham Maslow*

She first opened herself to the suggestions of others who might be able to help. She knew she was not alone. Others had gone through cancer, ovarian and otherwise, and survived. She spoke to psychologists, cancer patients, oncologists, meditation specialists, and some of the seniors she had taught at the center, from which she had taken an extended leave. Lena began to meditate, especially when she felt pain. She woke up in the morning focused not on hurrying to get things done, but on experiencing what the day had to tell her. She began keeping a journal. She found that her journal writing was not only a way to nurture herself and sit in the quiet of her soul, but it also provided a forum to question, hear answers, and celebrate the insight that was growing within her.

She then began to collect copies of works of art that moved her—Botticelli, van Gogh, Monet, and Goya. Friends would help collect them from the Internet or pick up poster versions, which Lena mounted in scrapbooks and on her apartment walls. The art was a constant reminder of the creativity she admired; creativity that was now a priority in her daily life. Lena was committed to draining the darkness from her body and her life. It would not control her. Being creative was an affront to the darkness, for it brought light into her day. With it, she took back control of her life. And with this creative spark came a profound realization— although darkness and pain were emanating from her physical, emotional, and spiritual wounds, they were also inspiring her to *do more, feel more, create more.* She began to see those competing effects, and she was determined to give the upper hand to the forces that elevated her life.

Lena began opening herself to spontaneous prayer. If something moved her, whether it was a phone call of support, a poem, something she'd written in her journal, the memory of her mom, or watching the elderly in their movement class, she would close her eyes and bless the moment as a gift to her. A fellow cancer patient introduced her to guided imagery. Sometimes during a walk on the beach or lying on her apartment floor, the new friend would guide her through the process, which included imagining a ball of light that would move into the dark recesses of her body, through her arms and legs, her chest and abdomen, shining a healing illumination that would then spread throughout her limbs. Lena became so proficient that she could guide herself through the journey, and in the process hear a *voice* within her wounds urging her forward with a positive energy.

In addition, Lena fashioned a values list, prioritizing what was truly important in the process of living. She found herself focusing less on future plans and more on cherishing the here and now. She gave herself permission to complain, and reminded herself that it did not mean she wasn't being strong. Endurance became something she valued. It was itself a form of courage. She came to value gentleness within herself, and felt the spiritual healing that came from the collective love of others.

In fact, feeling connected to family, friends, fellow cancer patients and survivors, as well as those, like her mom, who had succumbed to cancer, became part of how she came to understand God. God was in that collective love she realized. God was in the creativity with which she approached her wounds. God was in her intolerance for her own suffering, the agitation at times that poured out in her journal. God was also in that ball of light that passed through her body when she meditated with guided imagery, and God was the *sacred* part of her wound that beckoned her not only with hope, but with the certainty that she *mattered*. She was not alone.

When I met up with Lena, she had completed a long series of chemotherapy sessions. Her baldness was merely a part of her now, and she wasn't the least bit self-conscious about it. Her serenity seemed to come from a place deep within her. Lena explained to me that she saw the resources and poetry inside her soul as the *sacred* part of her wounded body and injured spirit. It had, in some ways, made her feel both more alive and more whole, if such a thing could be imagined.

Lena died three months later. She had touched not only her family and friends with inspiration, but also the elderly in her movement classes, the children with whom she danced, medical personnel, and other cancer patients alike. She had truly given birth to hope and healing in the gifts she bestowed to everyone in her life.

And, of course, she had blessed me. She taught me lessons that continue to unfold. Meeting Lena had turned into a living and moving discourse on a human being's ability to cut through the negative elements of a serious illness, drain them of their power, and find the *sacred* elements that transform living. Lena had showed so many that suffering can raise one's awareness of what is real and what is not. She was proof of the reality that the *core belief* of one's own worth is crucial to living a life with affirmation and grace. Most important, she taught me that God can be found speaking from within our wounds. She showed me the *sacred within the pain.*

I never did find out the identity of the anonymous caller who had phoned me those three months earlier. But one part of the caller's message kept playing over and over in my mind: "*It would mean a great deal if you could visit her . . .*" What I didn't know then is that what the mysterious woman had *really* meant was that meeting Lena would mean a great deal to *me.*

By the way, do you remember my mentioning that this mystery female caller had an accent? Some time after these events, I discovered that Lena's mom had been an immigrant to this country from Hungary.

Maybe it *is* true: God works in mysterious ways.

———

Lena wanted to share all that she had learned about her wounds, including what she'd come to learn about God, because when you've found that the *sacred* can be more powerful than the *profane* you want the world to know about it. People who have struggled with their pain and found a blessing within it have a much fuller idea about life's meaning than those who've never known such suffering. That doesn't make such people better, of course. No one would wish to be diagnosed with ovarian cancer, or lose a child or suffer anything so devastating. But given the wound inflicted upon her, Lena chose what that heartache was going to mean in her life. And she chose well.

Remember, Lena's initial *core belief* following her surgery was that no one really cared. She was alone, powerless, without hope. Keeping busy concealed her feelings of helplessness and fear. Lena's core belief gave rise to her anger at God and her family and friends, and an attempt to alienate those who wanted to draw close to her. But when she took the time to open herself to the truth, she was able to break away from that core belief. She was not alone. People cared about her desperately, especially her father. While life isn't always fair, she recognized that hope could grow out of the very pain that sought to destroy her. And she learned more about her own abilities and self-worth than she believed possible.

Lena came to see that she wasn't isolated or marginalized—rather that, wounds and all, she mattered profoundly. This alternative belief opened her to the collective love outside of herself and the passionate choices waiting to be tapped within her. Most significantly, her transformation allowed her to drain the negative energy associated with her pain and discover the *sacred* affirmation that was her blessing.

Using one's wounding experiences to sanctify living, to elevate one's consciousness of what is possible and important in life, is an essential element in *making meaning* out of our pain. Each of us has the power to take *Step Three*, to drain away negative, destructive messages within us and face the light of our own potential. It's a choice we can make consciously when we arm ourselves with an alternative belief that affirms the reality that *we matter profoundly*.

———

THE TASK

Now let us monitor our *core beliefs.*

As stated earlier in this chapter, Dr. Beck's work on Cognitive Therapy has shown that our thought processes are tied to events that have happened to us and that we use to determine how to view the world and our place in it. In other words, what we *believe* comes by way of our experience. Since being wounded is an integral part of our life's experience, we can state: *wounds = experience = our belief system.* For example, the wound Lena felt with the death of her mother *could* have led her to stay bitter about her own inability to help. This helplessness could have poisoned Lena's view of what she had to offer others. Our task in *Step Three* is to examine the core beliefs associated with our particular wound and find what poisoned distortions exist there. It is these *profane* messages that we seek to drain away.

In your journal, create three headings:

⚘ *The Wound*
⚘ *What It Says About Me*
⚘ *How It Makes Me Feel*

For example, you might record under *The Wound,* "I was rejected by my husband after twenty years of marriage." What this may say about your current condition, as a result of the wound, is, "I'm not lovable; no one wants me; I have little worth." This would be a *core belief.* You might then go on to record that this belief makes you feel *depressed, alienated, angry, hopeless.* Be sure to use words that identify how you are feeling as a result of your own wound. (Of course, your wound may not have to do with rejection, but you can apply the feelings described above to your specific situation.)

Let me encourage you now to consider the possibility of an *alternative belief* based on contrary evidence you yourself can provide. In this case, rather than accepting the core belief that you are *unlovable* and that *no one wants to be with you,* might you not examine your life carefully and find evidence to suggest that *you are valued, others enjoy your company* and *want to be with you?* Starting on a new page, under the heading *Alternative Belief,* list those experiences that might provide evidence that your core belief is *not entirely true:* "My colleague laughed out loud this morning when I shared a funny story with her; my friends told me they really enjoyed having dinner with me; being part of the planning committee makes me feel useful and connected and they seem to actually respect my ideas."

Record on another page in your journal the same headings as before: *The Wound, What It Says About Me, How It Makes Me Feel.* The wound you experienced is a constant. Now, however, try stating an alternative belief and the more positive attributes that the evidence suggests—you are lovable, capable of joy, people show an interest in you, you still have dreams and aspirations. Might it also be clear from the observations you have recorded that you have *the capacity for optimism,* you are *connected to others,* and that *love is still possible?* (It could also begin to dawn on you, with an alternative belief that embraces self-love, that if someone chooses not to see your worth and shows a capacity to reject you, then there is something *sacred* missing in that person. Why would you wish to be in a relationship like that?)

When you have fashioned an alternative belief, based on your real, everyday life experience, you will, as the apex of *Step Three,* link your suffering to an alternative, positive, and *sacred* belief, thereby draining the wound of negative power, the *profane* of your pain.

If you cannot find your way to these positive affirmations, then you may still be stuck in a negative core belief. It may take some time. That's all right. Collect the evidence. Be more aware of the possibility of alternative beliefs. And know that you have the opportunity to *create* new evidence with the way you live life daily. Keep working at it. Remember— *you are worth it.*

Draining away that which leads to a *profane existence* marked by a distorted view of our lives allows us to consider the meaning our wounds can have in the way we approach life. Each of us possesses a deep desire to grow. We want to elevate our understanding of our needs and embrace our higher selves. We want to see that something good can emerge from our suffering, that pain need not only con-

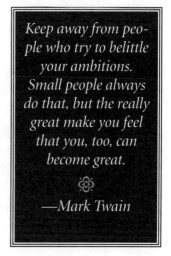

Keep away from people who try to belittle your ambitions. Small people always do that, but the really great make you feel that you, too, can become great.

—Mark Twain

tain darkness but can also shed light. It is this light that exists for each and every one of us when we go in search of the *sacred* within our individual wounds.

THE RITUAL

This ceremony incorporates composing an original prayer and the use of guided imagery.

Lie down where you are comfortable. You may choose to have soft music playing or simply bathe in the silence. Concentrate on the breath that is moving through your body. Be aware of its rhythm and flow. Listen to its journey and follow its progress from your head, down through your chest, your arms, your abdomen, your pelvis, and down through your legs and out your feet. Allow yourself to accompany that breath as it moves through your being with freedom, relaxing you in its journey of hope, for each breath is a gift of life. As Lena did when she gave blessings of appreciation, spontaneously create a prayer that encompasses the experience of today. Be sure it includes recognition for something that has *blessed you,* or for which you give thanks.

Now imagine yourself as you are today meeting up with a much older version of yourself, twenty, thirty, fifty years in the future. You slowly walk toward one another in a field of light. There is a sweetness in the air, and the sound of your breath carries you forward. You look at one another, studying each other's features. This older version of yourself has been around, has had many more experiences, has survived many more wounds, and is still standing. There is so much you want to ask. So much you want to know. And as you open your mouth to inquire of your older self, a finger moves to his or her lips, quieting you.

Still, you have questions. You open your mouth once more to speak, and again your older self quiets you with a gentle smile. And then, at that moment, your older self encompasses you in a healing embrace. This embrace feels like God's embrace, warm and gentle and supremely comforting. And the pain that has coursed through your body is draining right out of you. And the darkness that has taken up residence in your wounds is being replaced by a luminescence that shines pure love right through you. It's the way you've always wanted to be held. You are resting in your own arms, blessed by the soul of your own experience.

Rest there for as long as you wish, and when you are done, gather up that light within you and bring it back to the present. It is the gift you give yourself today.

THE GIFT

We affirm the miracles of self-knowledge that emerge when we find the *sacred* within our pain:

> ❀ I realize now that my wounds offer *more* than I might have imagined. They can liberate me from *core beliefs* that have distorted my self-image and proven detrimental to my growth.
>
> ❀ I am capable of draining the *profane* and negative influences from my wound and uncovering the affirmation that lies within it.

❀ I may not be able to choose the pain I've gone through, but I *do* have the power to determine what this wound is going to *mean* for my life.

Lena died all too young. Most of us do not have wounds that will threaten us as Lena's did. But even in her pain, she inspired many to grow creatively and passionately through the experience of being wounded. She found what she truly valued and shifted her priorities to those that sanctified and elevated her life.

We now recognize that we, too, can allow the waters of our own positive priorities to wash across our wound, naming the sacredness of what we have taken from our pain, allowing it to push away the negative aspects of hate, anger, fear, and apathy, and sit, ever still, in the resulting blessing.

It is the gift that emerges from having gone successfully in search of the *sacred* and having found that the miracle of its existence resides within our own souls and our own hearts.

And, yes, even in our wounds.

We have now expanded our consciousness to find the *sacred* within our pain. This propels us toward *Step Four,* where we will come to embrace the success-producing *wisdom of our wounds.*

STEP FOUR

ACCEPTING THE WISDOM: The Birth of the Sacred

*People are like stained-glass windows. They sparkle and shine
when the sun is out, but when the darkness sets in, their
true beauty is revealed only if there is a light from within.*
—Elisabeth Kübler-Ross

THE MEDITATION
*Now that I am able to see the sacred
The path of my steps has revealed
Let me now embrace the precious insights—
the wisdom of my wounds
the learning in my pain
the truth within my life's experience.*

*May I weave from the tapestry of their light
A garment of perception
A raiment of understanding
And may my welcome of this wisdom
Lead me ever further
along my journey so I may
renew my spirit
revive my vision
redeem my purpose.*

———

In the last step, we endeavored to drain the *profane* elements of our pain that can instill in us *core beliefs* that restrict our growth and success. We discovered in our wounds the existence of the *sacred*, born of a higher consciousness, to which *Step Three* awakened us. *Step Four*, Accepting the Wisdom, leads us to the awareness that there is, indeed, learning attached to our suffering. It is in recognizing the *wisdom of our wounds* that we begin to *transform pain into possibility*, imbuing the wound with a *sacred* spirit that becomes a touchstone to success.

In her landmark work *On Death and Dying*, Elisabeth Kübler-Ross speaks of the five stages human beings must go through when faced with grief and loss: denial, anger, bargaining, depression, and acceptance. Grief and loss, however, are not limited to the realms of death and dying. They are experienced with the breakup of a relationship, a child's involvement with drugs, or the loss of dignity that can come with bankruptcy. We may be stuck in the rut of just "going along," living a life of quiet desperation or one that is simply low-grade miserable. Perhaps our wounds have mounted up, and we've stopped fighting for ourselves and our spirit. We may be stuck in the stage of denial, guilt, or anger, and have yet to pass through all of the stages of grief and loss.

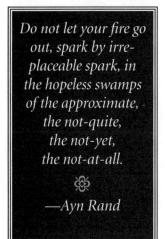

Do not let your fire go out, spark by irreplaceable spark, in the hopeless swamps of the approximate, the not-quite, the not-yet, the not-at-all.

—*Ayn Rand*

If we are in one of these earlier stages right now, the wisdom of our wounds will be more difficult to recognize and accept. However, we've come this far, so clearly we *want* to see it. It may take passing through Kübler-Ross's other stages to come to a point where we're ready to discern that this wisdom exists.

By accepting our suffering and sorrow, I don't mean to suggest that we ought to embrace the idea that we were *meant* to be in pain, that we somehow deserved to be. That would be a destructive form of acknowledgment. Rather, given that our wound is already part of our landscape, we must recognize that we possess knowledge as a *result* of the experience, and when we are ready, we can move on and *use* it. This is not a gift with which we are born; nor is it a birthright. Rather, it is wisdom based on experience, which is why I call it a *life-right*.

When we are ready to embrace this acceptance stage, we will also come to see the inherent wisdom in our pain. It is at this moment that we first glimpse the birth of our ability to take loss and transform it into motivation for success. Kübler-Ross, in the quote that leads off this *Fourth Step*, speaks of realizing our true beauty in the darkness of our lives. The light within us, she says, provides stark relief to that darkness. But what *light* is this?

It is the light of our learning—the wisdom of our wounds.

When I consider those who have accepted the knowledge they received from their pain and transformed their lives as a result, I think of bicyclist and humanitarian Lance Armstrong. He made world headlines in Paris on July 25, 1999, with perhaps the most stunning comeback ever in the history of sports, winning the Tour de France (an amazing achievement he would repeat in 2000, 2001, and yet again in 2002!). And he did so after having conquered a devastating medical obstacle. Through his famed battle with and victory over testicular cancer, Armstrong found personal and professional triumph. As he rode his bike to victory in the grueling French Alps, he was proof of the success that can be inspired by life's suffering. His recognition that his pain contained wisdom that could help him grow even stronger led him to understand that, in the bigger and broader scheme of things, he was already a champion—a champion at living life. Armstrong has described his bout with cancer as "a special wake-up call." At the victory line in Paris, he was quoted as saying, "If there's one thing I say to those who use me as their example, it's that if you ever get a second chance in life, you've got to go all the way."

THE SILVER CLOUD

One of the ways we come to an acceptance of the wisdom of our traumatic experiences is in our approach to new challenges that come our way. In the past, certain life challenges may have rendered us helpless and terrified, but we now know that there are insights to be found in experiences that test our lives. With this new wisdom, we can begin to use a tool that allows us to restate challenges. This is a tool of the imagination, referred to by cognitive-behavioral therapists as a "cognitive reframe."

Let me give you an example. A good friend of mine named Bill has a sister, Lori, who is blind. They are both middle-aged, and their parents are deceased. Bill is a working professional with a busy personal life, but he tries hard to be there for his sister. A young woman hired to assist Lori takes her to appointments,

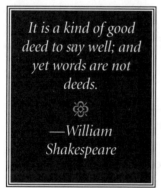

It is a kind of good deed to say well; and yet words are not deeds.

—William Shakespeare

restaurants, and the like. One day recently, however, Lori had been feeling under the weather and was set to go to the doctor. At the same time, her young helper was called away to a family emergency. Overwhelmed, she called Bill in tears: she was all alone, not feeling well, and with him tied up there was no one to help her. She began to enumerate all the obstacles facing the blind, when suddenly Bill interrupted her by reframing her situation. "Wait a minute," he said. "You mean you get to go to your doctor on your *own*? Hey, that is fantastic. You've never done that before. Look what you get to do on your own power,

Lori! And me, I get to watch you accomplish this—*wow*! I am so proud of you. And you know what? You can *do* this."

Bill is a passionate guy, and he meant every word. He *did* think it was an opportunity for his sister to grow. And that passion was empowering and contagious. His sister heard the excitement in his voice, the affirmation it provided of her own abilities and, suddenly, she could see it and recognize the strength she had possessed all along. She was positively galvanized by her own potential.

Bill had managed to calmly take what his sister had seen as a raging squall that threatened to upend the ship of her well-being, and reframe it as a *silver cloud*. He had diminished the size of the obstacle, downsizing it from "menacing" to "manageable." But he had done something more—he had shown that this obstacle, this threatening storm, had a silver lining. It could be used as a motivator to accept the wisdom he knew Lori possessed: she was capable of success on her own. As a result of Bill's acknowledgment of his sister's limitations, and his simultaneous belief that she could achieve a higher level of autonomy, Lori was able to move past the fear and false certainty of "I can't do this."

In the past, we may have said to ourselves (and everyone else in our path), "If she dies, if I get divorced, if I'm fired, if I miscarry—I would collapse. I wouldn't be able to go on." But for thousands of years, people have buried parents and loved ones, seen relationships dissolve, experienced the unspeakable pain of losing a child, faced frightening illnesses. Those who have survived are the ones who not only moved through the stages of grief to acceptance, but who used this evolution to recognize the wisdom born of their trauma in meeting life's challenges successfully. We can, too.

We will not only survive, though. We will draw on the wisdom of our wounds to take concrete action—to honor our loved ones who die, to create healthier relationships, to find a more meaningful and satisfying job, to find a way to channel our quest for parenthood into meaningful choices that can celebrate our dream in an alternative way. We are able to do this because we will be ready to identify the lessons our suffering is ready to teach us. And we *will* do so when we come to accept this wisdom with clarity and resolve. When we confront old wounds or face the possibility of new ones, it is our *learned experience* that can help turn them into *silver clouds,* diminishing the threat while providing an opportunity to grow. In New England, where we know from clouds, I have seen since childhood how clouds can obscure the light—but can also act like a spotlight, highlighting details and opportunities in life that we may otherwise miss.

I was walking with my wife, Bonnie, in a lovely Massachusetts coastal town when she observed the cloudy and gray day all around us. A child of California, she grew up on a steady diet of blue skies and cloudless nights. She says that you begin to take it for granted. But being from Vermont, I never did. Weather there comes in all kinds of permutations. I shared with her my view that when days are full of sunshine and the sky is one big blue heaven stretching out above us, it's easy to lose one's concentration. Our earthly and immediate concerns can get lost below such perfection. Cloudy days, however, always focus my attention back down to where I live. The gray clouds seem to beckon me to look around and notice what I might otherwise have missed. In so doing, I can transform them into *silver clouds*, as I consciously shrink the size of their potential threat and concentrate on my opportunity to see beauty right in front of me. It was at that moment that we both became aware of the many colored doors on the houses of the street where we were strolling. It was actually a neighborhood celebrating itself, each door unique to those dwelling within the home. Bonnie looked at me, grinning from ear to ear with this newfound appreciation—really, she said, she'd never even noticed them!

There are a lot of things worthy of our attention that we might not notice until our wounds give us that wake-up call. Reframing a challenging situation into a *silver cloud*, diminishing its severity and allowing it to focus us, permits that wake-up to center our attention. Otherwise the size of our pain is distorted, leaving us with the fear and panic that comes with being overwhelmed. At such moments, it is *we* who are diminished.

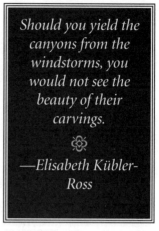

> *Should you yield the canyons from the windstorms, you would not see the beauty of their carvings.*
>
> —*Elisabeth Kübler-Ross*

If we are unable to accept the lessons our wounds have to teach us, then it may be due to our failure to *reframe the storm* in our minds. If we cannot make out the learning in the pain, then we cannot give birth to its *sacred* message. We're meandering through a depression caused by a meaningless relationship and, suddenly, our world is turned upside down by terrorists at the World Trade Center. *Can we really justify maintaining the status quo of our own loneliness in light of these events?* No. We deserve better for ourselves. *Step Four* shows how, by accepting the wisdom of our wounds, we can reframe pain into a *silver cloud* that can help us focus on attaining all we deserve.

What is crucial to understand here—to be crystal clear about if we're to move on—is that it's *never* the initial wounding experience that is responsible for continued emotional pain and sorrow in our lives. Rather, it's what we have come to tell ourselves about it. This is precisely how the core beliefs operate, as we learned in *Step Three*. Like my friend's blind sister, we may face a challenging situation that our core beliefs have convinced us we cannot handle: "I can't start over now that she's gone; I was lucky to find one person to love; I can't push my luck." "I can't ask for help with my addiction, no one thinks I'm worth it." "I can't handle you getting sick, when my mother died I was a basket case."

But in reframing what we tell ourselves, we have the power to transform our responses to life's challenges. This transformation is made possible because we have become aware of the wisdom we've accrued from our Sacred Wounds. Recognizing the wisdom that is our *life-right* gives birth to new and insightful responses that are *sacred*, because they help lead us to growth.

REFRAMING THE NEGATIVE

*H*armful images burst forth naturally when we are wounded. Reframing these negative associations is a key part of accepting the wisdom of our wounds. Using the *silver cloud* switch interrupts our old destructive ways of doing and thinking. We can learn to say to our old selves: *"You call it a catastrophe, I call it a challenge."*

For example, we may come to believe that we have nothing to offer others who have been similarly hurt. The destructive, *profane* elements of our past wounds might warn us to avoid contact with further pain. But it is the wisdom of our wounds that can produce an alternative belief: by allowing the light of our compassion into another's life, we become a channel for illumination. By giving to others, we strike the very match that brings illumination into our own lives.

> They might not need
> me; but they might.
> I'll let my head be
> just in sight;
> A smile as small as
> mine might be
> Precisely their
> necessity.
>
> ⚘
>
> —Emily Dickinson

Finding light through our wounds is the purpose of *Step Four*. We must reach the stage where we are prepared to accept this offering. Kübler-Ross speaks of acceptance as the final stage in dealing with grief and loss. But I envision the act of healing and growth as a sacred circle of *steps* through which we return not to our initial grief, but to our initial—now changed—selves. By drawing on the experience of our trauma, we put those insights to work for us in our mission to claim our true potential. The Oglala Sioux imagine the life journey as a *sacred hoop*. If one part of the journey is missing, the sacred hoop is incomplete. It may become torn by loss and grief, it may lose a segment through death or depression. To restore the hoop is to restore the sacredness of purpose and spirit that belongs in our life. *Accepting the wisdom* of our wounds is, therefore, a *life-right*, an act of restoring ourselves to our true potential. It is making use of all our parts, whether wounded or not.

Our wounds are thus as much a part of who we are as is the air we breathe and the dreams we dream. In taking *Step Four* and accepting the wisdom of our wounds, we also accept the knowledge that confirms that our wounds are knit into the fabric of our spirit. Their wisdom is *sacred* because it elevates our growth and sets us on a path to empowering our future. Noted Hollywood director Jonathan Lynn and his wife, Rita, a British psychoanalyst, were wounded in an IRA bombing at a London airport some years ago. They remember keenly the shattering of their lives. But as they dealt with the trauma of their life-threatening experience they came to a new and powerful decision that they were going to live each day richly and with a commitment they had hitherto not known they possessed. The painful experience is today still a part of them. Yet so is the elevated energy and affirmation it produced, an insight they have employed to empower their lives, crowning them with creativity, humor, and passion. Such is the gift in accepting the wisdom of their wounds.

———

I'd like to share with you the story of a couple who seemed to be living a charmed life. Suddenly, they experienced a devastating loss that left their dreams in tatters. It would only be by accepting the wisdom of their wounds that together they could give birth to the *sacred* realization that success comes of discovering the true priorities of our hearts.

Rick and Sara's Story

*R*ick and Sara were inseparable from the moment they met during their freshman year at Williams College, in Massachusetts. He was considering a theater major at the time, and she was in one of his acting classes. They were drawn to each other right away. Sara liked the fact that he was carrying a book of poetry by e. e. cummings—and, better yet, she loved that he had actually read it. Rick was attracted to the fact that she didn't hide her natural beauty behind makeup, and he loved the way her laughter rolled out of her throat with absolute abandon. Before the fall semester was over, Rick and Sara had begun a full-blown romance. Four years later, they were married and expected, as we all do, to live happily ever after.

Their wedding took place the day immediately after their graduation so that their families could get two celebrations for the price of one. During the reception there were a bundle of toasts, many touching on the glorious future awaiting the bride and groom, and the gorgeous children Rick and Sara would surely have one day. There was talk of Rick's plan to attend law school after having had a two-year flirtation with the theater, and Sara's dream of becoming a playwright. After a honeymoon in the Virgin Islands, they settled in the city that never sleeps, New York.

While Sara taught English in an Upper West Side private school, Rick received his law degree at New York University. Upon graduation he went to work for a midtown law firm, and Sara quit teaching in order to enter a graduate program in playwriting at the New School. They were living the life they had always dreamed of: exploring Manhattan's rich cultural offerings, jogging in Central Park, heading to New England for weekend getaways in time for the fall foliage.

By the time they reached their late twenties, they began talking seriously about their plans for a family. Sara's idea of perfection was to have two babies—a boy and a girl if possible. Rick had a slightly grander concept, which Sara had long known. He came from a family of four boys, so a big family had always been his ideal. They settled on a compromise they could both live with—three children. The hope was that they could remain in the Manhattan brownstone they adored until the babies were old enough for school. Then Rick might transfer to the Boston offices of his firm, allowing them to raise their children in a more suburban setting.

While they were in pregnancy mode in 1995, Sara began work on a new play that dealt with an expectant couple and the comedic angst that comes with finding *just the right name*. As she envisioned it, the play would bring in each of the characters' family backgrounds, the dreams of the husband and wife when they first pictured being parents, and the roller-coaster ride of anticipating an event that would change all of their lives. But what ended up changing *their* lives was quite the opposite of Sara's three-act play.

They had been trying to get pregnant for five months. Sara began to grow concerned, but she was assured that it typically took couples their age about six months to a year to become pregnant. Some of Rick's male colleagues suggested that maybe he was "doing it" too often. "You don't want to dilute that source, buddy," one joked. But Sara and Rick had no problem concentrating on the fertile times of the month. As the months ticked by, however, both Sara and Rick grew more anxious. The following September, after trying for a full year, they decided to make an appointment with Sara's obstetrician/gynecologist, Dr. Kendall. After a careful examination, the doctor assured them they had no cause for alarm. Nevertheless, she suggested that they each be tested for problems that might affect their fertility. Rick discovered that this meant having to masturbate into a plastic cup at a fertility lab, while the sound of foot traffic abounded on the other side of the door. The test for sperm volatility and production confirmed he had healthy sperm function. At the same time, Sara went for a series of tests that also turned up no problems. They were both delighted.

More time went by, and still no baby. Why was it taking so long? After a year and a half of Sara's trying to get pregnant, Dr. Kendall arranged for her to undergo exploratory surgery to see if there was something wrong with her reproductive system that hadn't been detected in the lab tests. There was: both her ovaries were full of cysts. Dr. Kendall removed them, and put Sara on a regimen of the fertility drug Clomid to help stimulate ovulation.

Suddenly, sex became a highly regimented, almost scientific, activity. They had to time their intercourse down to the most fertile twelve hours in Sara's monthly cycle. Rick felt the pressure of performing, and Sara, hopeful as she was, found the joy of sex replaced by the fear that she wouldn't conceive. Maybe this time it will work, she thought each month. After a number of months went by, Sara went in for a postcoital test the morning after intercourse. It proved what the doctor had feared: Rick's sperm were immobile inside her. For some inexplicable reason, they could not survive inside her body.

At home that night, Rick witnessed for the first time the self-blame that had been eating away at his wife. "You would have been better off without me," she told him in tears. "I'm just damaged goods." Everything in their lives—school, the law degree, Rick's job, her MFA—it had all come so easily, Sara cried in anguish. "But now our luck's run out, Rick, and it's because of me—it's all my fault!" Sara must have apologized a thousand times that night. Rick took her in his arms as she cried herself to sleep, telling her again and again how much he loved her, assuring her they would work this out.

Dr. Kendall had referred them to a fertility specialist, Dr. Sorenson, and now Rick held Sara's hand tightly as they sat opposite Dr. Sorenson and listened to a description of more extreme courses of action such as artificial insemination, intrauterine insemination, and in-vitro fertilization. Dr. Sorenson explained that insurance companies do not usually cover fertility treatments. Intrauterine insemination would be under a thousand dollars, but in-vitro fertilization procedures can cost between eight and fifteen thousand dollars. After discussing their situation, they decided to try intrauterine insemination (IUI). The date was set for the IUI procedure; even with the doctor's caution about rates of success and the emotional ups and downs of the fertility process, Sara and Rick left his office feeling more hopeful than they had been in nearly two years. The idea of going through life without children was frightening. Finally, here was hope. During Sara's next ovulation, the two went into action. Rick provided the sperm that morning to Dr. Sorenson's lab technicians, who then "washed" it and prepared a concentrated sample to be used in the procedure. Rick joined Sara, and Dr. Sorenson injected the sperm directly into the uterus.

At work, Rick had been more anxious than usual, and the partners in the law firm had noticed he had been cutting back his hours. Rick assured them that he was handling everything, and that he and Sara expected some good news any day. When it was discovered ten days later that the IUI hadn't worked, however, Rick called in sick, and he and Sara took a country drive to Connecticut. Sara wasn't able to enjoy the scenery; all she could think of was starting the next procedure.

That night Sara lay awake, watching Rick sleep fitfully, and thinking about the past two years. She recognized that she'd become obsessed with getting pregnant and that nothing else seemed to matter. She hadn't worked on her play in nearly a year. The quest for a child had completely taken over her life. She read books about fertility and pregnancy nonstop, and now all she could focus on was the next procedure. That was everything. She couldn't sleep.

Meanwhile, Rick was beginning to feel isolated. He had been so concerned with Sara's frame of mind that he hadn't allowed himself to feel his own sense of failure. Four months later, after almost two and a half years of heartache, it caught up with him. He was getting out of a cab in front of FAO Schwarz on Fifty-ninth Street, heading for a meeting with a client. Suddenly, the sight of a couple with their two children carrying bundles of Christmas presents out of the store struck him like a bolt of lightning to the heart. Rick crossed the street, slipped into the park, found a vacant bench, and broke down, crying his dreams into the cold afternoon air.

After five unsuccessful attempts with the IUI procedure, Dr. Sorenson recommended in-vitro fertilization (IVF). Even though the insurance company assured the fertility specialists that they would handle a good portion of the procedure, the doctor had still asked Rick and Sara to take out a loan for a deposit in case the insurance money didn't come through. He apologized, explaining that this was standard procedure. For the next four months, Rick faithfully administered the hormone shots that would assist Sara in producing enough eggs for the IVF procedure. She had numerous ultrasounds, and on the first try they harvested seven good eggs. Three of them implanted immediately, but Sara didn't get pregnant. Several months later, they implanted the other four eggs and this time, something happened. Amazingly, Sara was pregnant—with twins! One minute they were running joyfully through Central Park, the next Rick and Sara were on the phone with both their families. The next day, Rick handed out bubble-gum cigars at the office and threw himself into his work with renewed passion. Sara took out her play and began writing again. Their life seemed back on track; they pinched one another in giddiness each morning.

A week and a half later, however, Sara woke up with cramps. Rick found her doubled over in the bathroom. Within hours, Sara miscarried. The two of them held each other on the floor; the pain was devastating. Neither of them could put into words their grief. They cried together, and, later, alone. As the weeks wore on with the promise of yet another procedure, Sara found herself railing at God in anger. "Why did you do this to me? I have so much love to give my baby. What difference does it make to the goddamn universe if you give me this gift? I deserve to be a mother, you bastard. I deserve it. . . ." Her tears seemed unstoppable.

Over the course of four and a half years, they struggled with the reality of childlessness. Rick and Sara sought out couples counseling to deal with their grief and the dangerous wedge growing between them, the emotional barrier that often arises when something sacred dies. The dream of having a family was integral to who they were as individuals and as a couple. How could they live with this wound? They heard, read, and felt it all: "This is God's way of telling you that you shouldn't be parents." "You can always adopt." "Maybe you can hire someone else to carry your baby—would that bother you?" They were cautioned by a therapist to say no to baby-focused activities that made the pain more acute. This meant avoiding the birthday parties of their friends' children, baby showers, and baby namings. But they couldn't avoid the sight of babies as they took their evening strolls in Central Park, and their life together was a constant reminder of what was missing.

Rick was adamant against surrogacy. They had both heard too many horror stories about surrogates turning on the parents at the last minute and claiming the babies for themselves. Sara couldn't bring herself to discuss adoption, because it reminded her of her own inability to bring a new life into the world.

As the year 2000 approached, the whole world was getting millennium fever. Rick had failed to make partner at the firm because he had missed too much time over the years, and though his employers were sympathetic, they nevertheless questioned his priorities. On the morning he learned he wouldn't be promoted, he went outside, lost in emotion, and began to walk from his offices in midtown Manhattan. Before he knew it he was all the way through Central Park and approaching Spanish Harlem. He was taking stock of where he was in his life. With his law firm already wondering about his commitment, now it was his turn to do the same. He walked for hours, his mind filling with images and dreams and the voice of his wounds. The never-ending grief had taken its toll on their marriage, and Rick couldn't remember the last time their lovemaking had been a loving experience. On top of this, they had wiped out their savings and they were living on loans and near bankruptcy. He had carried an image of Sara in tears for nearly five years. Her sorrow had eaten away at the laughter that had first drawn him to her. Her self-blame and anger at the world had infected him with an overpowering hopelessness. His priorities weren't straight? What *were* his priorities?

That night Rick returned to the brownstone to find Sara on the floor of their apartment, rocking herself with sadness. And the sight of what she had become, what *they* had become on their obsessive quest to create a baby, filled him with a sudden clarity that rose like a cry from his soul. "I can't stand this anymore, Sara. Look at you. You weren't meant to live a life of tears and anger and depression. When I met you at Williams, your laughter was everywhere. We were the golden couple, because everywhere we went we found that life made us smile; we took the joy in. But we haven't known joy in years. We've been living inside our own pain for too long, and it's dark in here. And it's cold. I want your smile back. I want us to find joy again. My heart breaks for everything you've gone through, that we've gone through. But we have to take back our lives!" Sara cried out at him in anger, rising and beating his chest with her fists in a fit of grief and rage, before collapsing in tears into his arms.

Rick held her with all the love he possessed. "Listen to me, Sara," he spoke soothingly. "We haven't wasted a moment. I wouldn't trade away any of what we've been through." She blinked up into his face. "What do you mean? We've been miserable. . . ." "Yes." He nodded with a soft smile. "But we've been given the most precious gift of all. Today my law firm refused to make me a partner. They questioned my priorities. But don't you see? Everything we've experienced together has taught me that they're absolutely wrong. And so are we. My priority is you and our marriage. It always has been. I can't bear to think we won't be parents. I've dreamed of this baby just as long as you have. But you know what? I'll live. I know I will. But I could never live without loving you." Sara sobbed into his chest, and they held each other like that for hours.

That night they made love with a passion and tenderness neither of them had felt in years. They stayed up until dawn, talking about letting go of dreams and building new ones, about knowing that they had succeeded at deepening their love for one another by having gone through all the heartache. They spoke of accepting this pain, and of knowing that they had and always would put each other first. Sara said she understood now what it meant to share the ugliest and most challenging moments and know that your partner will not leave you. Rick explained that he had come to see that a woman didn't have to give birth to be a woman. She had to give a more precious gift— her love.

Rick and Sara felt a different kind of creation as the dawn kissed the city that day. It was the rebirth of their commitment to each other. Each had been tested by their shared wounds. And each had found in the wisdom of their suffering a knowledge that would bless their future. It was the kind of knowledge that not only helped them hold fast to their priorities in life, but opened them to a new concept of success that had less to do with human biology and much more to do with reproducing the love that's born in our hearts again and again.

Rick and Sara spoke off and on about adoption over the next year and a half. And then came the shocking blow of September 11, 2001, when the twin towers of the World Trade Center were reduced to rubble, taking thousands of lives with them. Like so many others, they were profoundly affected. They now felt a knowledge growing in them from the pain the city and the nation were suffering. Talking about dreams, even new and different ones, is just that, they realized—talk. This was a time for action. They could still be parents and give their love to a child. And even though it hadn't been their choice to begin with, making the choice for a family was a *sacred* one, for it was born of their suffering. Four months after the attacks in New York, Rick and Sara returned from China, where they had adopted a little girl.

Now Sara knew what to do with her play. The characters would go through many obstacles to fulfill their quest to be a family. And they would decide on a name for their child based not on their own respective ancestors, but on what was created out of the wisdom of the wounds they had shared in giving that child a home. This is why the little pillow in the crib in their apartment greets their daughter with the message "This Home Belongs to Hope."

———

Rick and Sara discovered that recognizing the wisdom of their wounds could help to heal their sorrow, and lead them to a renewal of their love. In *accepting this wisdom,* they not only found their way out of the darkness and into the light of a new beginning, but blessed that beginning with the birth of a new and *sacred* dream. They had taken a loss that might otherwise have destroyed their life together and transformed it into a *silver cloud* that reframed the future for them, giving them the insight to grow in closeness and in depth. In doing so they were able to see that success can be found on an alternative path, and that tri-

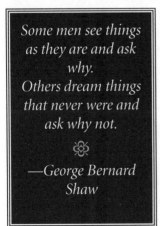

Some men see things as they are and ask why.
Others dream things that never were and ask why not.

❀

—George Bernard Shaw

umph can be achieved by knowing what's truly important and treasuring this wisdom.

We take a step toward succeeding in the great adventure of our lives by *accepting the wisdom* that comes along the way. Taking *Step Four,* we come to discover truths that can have a major impact on who we are and where we want to go by recognizing and accepting the lessons our pain produces. In reframing our suffering, we rewrite the messages we are sending our hearts, and arrive at an understanding that is also an affirmation—lessons are meant to be lived.

THE TASK

We have seen that one of the tools we can use to accept the wisdom of our wounds is a *cognitive reframe.* We take what look like violent storms and turn them into *silver clouds.* And by gaining knowledge about what constitutes life-threatening weather in our emotional and spiritual lives, we are capable of recognizing a cloud on the horizon as something manageable, something that needn't destroy our lives.

Think of a novice sailor who has never had experience at sea. He goes out with a seasoned captain and several accomplished seamen on a sporting expedition. En route, he becomes alarmed at the growing convergence of gray clouds on the horizon. Suddenly, there's a bolt of lightning thrown into the mix. By now he's shaking with fear, warning the captain that they had better turn back or risk being lost out in the massive sea. As the young sailor continues to scan the darkness in the cloud formations and notes several more lightning bolts, he

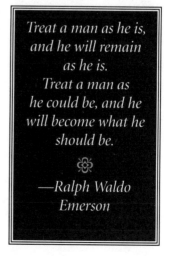

Treat a man as he is, and he will remain as he is.
Treat a man as he could be, and he will become what he should be.

⊛

—Ralph Waldo Emerson

works himself up into a state of frenzy. The captain smiles gently and pulls him aside. "Those clouds are moving in a southwest direction. Floaters, we call them. Sporadic lightning often accompanies them; we've seen it many times. A true storm would spread out north and west as well—this is a small pattern. Trust me, we're fine. Now c'mon over here, and learn how to handle the sail. That'll come in handy down the line." With that assurance, the sailor is able to go back to helping out on board instead of focusing on a fear that isn't based in reality.

We are that captain, seasoned by our past wounds. But we might continue to act the part of the novice sailor when confronted by life, forgetting what we know. The *silver cloud* reframe is a technique that can allow us to be in touch with the wisdom that can shrink the "overwhelming" obstacles in our path. By diminishing fear and putting life's challenges into perspective, we are also clearing a path to success that might otherwise appear blocked. It allows us access to the lessons that are our *life-right*.

Take time now to record in your journal answers to the following:

How can I make use of the *silver cloud* to diminish my fears so I can accept my wounds and move closer to the birth of my own potential? Is the success I want really impossible? Am I really unable to stand up, go out, handle a new situation, or is it the fear talking? Call up one of your fears. Describe it in all of its size, power, and significance. Now turn it into clouds by reframing its overwhelming nature, describing it in terms that are manageable and which you *know* to be true. For example:

- "I couldn't handle the situation" becomes, "I *prefer* not to handle it, but I *can*."
- "That experience was the end of my life" becomes, "It was a really unpleasant episode that I *survived*."
- "The diagnosis was like a tornado unleashing a path of destruction on my family and me" becomes, "It shook us

all up, and suddenly we saw what living every day fully really *means.*"

Our wounds teach us that clouds are manageable. The *silver cloud* has a lining that provides an opportunity for self-growth. Look for that opportunity, and accept the wisdom that can give birth to the potential within you.

THE RITUAL

When a child is born, depending on our religious or cultural orientation, we might celebrate with a baptism, a bris, some form of baby-naming ceremony, the planting of a tree, a bonfire, the lighting of candles, a contribution to charity, writing a poem, or toasting the baby's health.

When we accept the wisdom within our wounds and discover that our pain has given us lessons for our future, it is a birth as well. This is a birth that blesses us from within life—it is the birth of the *sacred.*

Celebrate this rebirth of your own possibilities with food, music, a toast, a poem. Meditate on it with the words that come to you in thanksgiving for finding the wisdom you have earned. And when you start to feel silly for toasting, planting, dancing, or whatever, just keep right on doing it. When we're not used to celebrating the good stuff that emerges out of the bad, we have to get used to doing so. So give yourself the room and the time to experience it. You've taken a powerful and positive step. You deserve the affirmation.

THE GIFT

We affirm the miracle of our newly acquired self-knowledge that is derived from the wisdom of our wounds:

❀ When I ask myself what I've learned from my pain, it allows my wounds to contribute lessons for my future.

❈ When I learn from my wounds' wisdom, I can transform
my pain. I can find a way to create different endings to the
stories I tell myself—and to the future I've yet to write.
❈ When I am willing to accept the wounds I've experienced
as *sacred* teachers, I have the capacity to grow.
❈ When I accept the wisdom born of past suffering, I realize
I can only do so with an open heart.

Step Five will teach us to claim the journey that the wisdom of
our wounds has helped to make possible, a heroic quest fashioned from the life lessons those wounds provide. This step will
lead us forward on the *precious path* to personal success. This is a
passageway that is created not despite but *because* of our Sacred
Wounds.

STEP FIVE

CLAIMING OUR JOURNEY: Discovering the Precious Path

The only real voyage of discovery consists not in seeking
new landscapes but in having new eyes.
—Marcel Proust

THE MEDITATION

On this precious path which is my life
may I send forth truth rather than lies,
the light of love rather than fear,
the seeds of hope rather than despair.

May I come to know teachings
As they are bestowed upon me
From the thicket of life's entanglements
and the flow of life's creative stream.

As I open the eyes of my soul
I will recognize the gifts
of my life's experience.
And in the awareness of this grace
let me more fully embrace
the journey that is mine alone to make.

———

In the last step we concentrated on *accepting* the wisdom of our wounded experiences, which now allows us to *open our eyes* and see before us a journey that beckons. The gift of understanding that is derived from our wounds prepares us to embark in a new direction. It is the knowledge we have acquired from our pain that makes possible an awareness of a pathway we have not previously discerned. This pathway may not at first be clear but, using the wisdom acquired in *Step Four,* we find we can now make out signposts pointing in its direction. And it must be stated—it is one thing to see the path, it's quite another actually to set foot on it. Setting foot on it means we claim it as our own *precious path*, which we know can lead us toward the success we want. It is now that we can take *Step Five,* read the signposts, and claim this journey as our own. It is now that we set ourselves on this pathway and use our new direction to unleash our truest potential.

The path offered by the wisdom of our wounds is often obscured and may not, at first, even look like or feel like a direction. To help us better understand the enlightening path, let us begin with a tale taken from Zen Buddhism. It is told in the form of a *koan*. Koans, literally meaning "cases," are seemingly unsolvable conundrums given to Zen students for study. The answer is not to be found through logic or thought, but rather through the *experience* itself. Let's examine one ourselves:

A monk said to Joshu, "I have just entered this monastery. Please teach me."

"Have you eaten your rice porridge?" asked Joshu.

"Yes, I have," replied the monk.

"Then you had better wash your bowl," said Joshu.

With this, the monk gained enlightenment.

For the Western mind, and even for some accustomed to Eastern thought, this koan is liable to produce nothing but bafflement. How on earth does anyone gain enlightenment by talking about porridge and washing bowls?! Or, to put it another way, where in this brief account is there any indication of how one gets from *there* to *here*? From "*Have you eaten your rice porridge?*" and the directive to "*wash your bowl*" to the threshold of profound illumination? The answer, as with so much else in life, is in the intangibles. The gift of direction is *within* the experience.

This koan reminds me of the time one of my ninth-grade students waited after class, eager to impress me. I was rushing from an Ethics and Values class to the student drama group I was directing, and hadn't noticed him until, pulling my things together, I found him blocking the door. He went on about how excited he was to study with me, and asked if I could give him a heads-up on how best to ace my course. I was going to be late for the rehearsal, so I am afraid I was rather abrupt. "I've got to go," I replied briskly. The student looked at me blankly, not moving. Then, closing his eyes, a smile began to form on his lips as he began nodding with growing comprehension. It was as if I'd just imparted to him the secret of life. Opening his eyes, he looked back at me with utter gratitude and replied, "*Right. I've got it now. Thanks.*"

To this day I'm still not sure I know just what the young man "got" or how he interpreted my need to rush away. His gleeful "I've got it now" expressed an understanding that seemed to come from nowhere—just as a Zen koan can seem to weave something from nothing.

THE MEANING OF THE KOAN

I came to understand the above koan only with the help of Zen teachings, and after some time spent sitting within the conundrum—"marinating" in it, as I call it. For the monks, breakfast is

Each morning we are born again. What we do today is what matters most.

—Buddha

always accompanied by silent meditation (*samadhi*). Thus, when Joshu asks, "*Have you eaten your rice porridge?*" he is asking the monk if he'd been able to accomplish this task while eating. The monk, understanding the hidden meaning of Joshu's apparently practical question, answers affirmatively. When Joshu then tells him, "*Then you had better wash your bowl,*" he is expressing the Zen way of being in the here and now. What's past is past. The enlightenment occurs within the monk's understanding of Joshu's meaning—once the porridge is eaten, the bowl should be washed, and he must go on to the next experience. It isn't about standing still and waiting for someone to fill you with enlightenment. Get on with your life and live it! To put it another way, we can *deal* with the past, but we ought not to *dwell* in it. The gift of this koan is in the understanding that we must *inhabit* the present and set foot in this new direction that can best serve us.

Pain and suffering are themselves "koans." On the surface, we may not readily recognize the precious path of enlightenment that heartache and anguish may open up for us. We might simply state the obvious: *pain is what it appears to be. It hurts, and it's awful. So where is the good in all that?* But like anything worth possessing in life, the journey we must make may require a greater effort from us to recognize it in order to match the potential of its reward.

THE QUEST FOR SUCCESS

*W*e are on a journey here. A quest, if you will. And as we know from our experiences with Arthurian legend—as well as *The Lord of the Rings, Star Wars,* or *Harry Potter,* for that matter—when it comes to a quest, nothing is simply what it appears to be. Joseph

Campbell was one of the twentieth century's great disseminators of the psychological wisdom of mythology. His extraordinary work on the topic of myths and archetypes includes an in-depth look at the "quest" narrative that is ubiquitous in the millions of stories about human nature. For Campbell, the quest is a journey of discovery or transformation. And the person on that quest becomes a hero because he

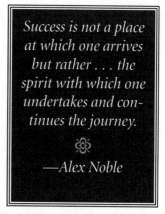

Success is not a place at which one arrives but rather . . . the spirit with which one undertakes and continues the journey.

—*Alex Noble*

or she, as a result of completing that journey, "comes to participate in life courageously and decently."

Our quest follows this *precious path* we are all on to discover and recover our Sacred Wounds. Each of us contains the seed of a hero yearning to live with courage and decency as a result of our many varied and amazing journeys. In order for that heroic seed to flower, however, we must first fertilize it with the gifts of discovery contained within our wounds. These gifts nourish our positive attitude toward life, what we want to accomplish on our journey, and how capable we are of getting there. They have a *procreative* effect on our soul. They not only nurture our own growth, but can reveal how we, in turn, can help nurture the world around us through the courage and decency of our actions, as we will see in the following step.

This is the basis for *Step Five.* In learning to recognize the precious path provided by our Sacred Wounds, we can claim our journey as a heroic quest for meaning and the success it can engender. As we've seen, our inability or unwillingness to deal with what has hurt us in the past, or is harming us right now, keeps this pathway out of sight and out of reach. Joseph Campbell put it this way: "Every failure to cope with a life situation must be laid, in the end, to a restriction of consciousness." It is this "restriction of consciousness" which increases the volatility and intensity of painful experiences, and this, in turn, withholds from us the direction of comfort and inspiration that waits in vain to be realized. A life that cannot recognize and act upon its own potential is destined to drown in a sea of regret. "Regrets," observes Campbell, "are illuminations come too late."

THE "WHO" AND "HOW" OF OUR LIFE'S JOURNEY

*T*hose of us moving through the *nine steps* are determined *not* to live the unrealized life. The direction that our wounds provide is there to be found now, not on some distant day when there may be little we can do to make use of it. I have a vivid recollection of being called to the hospital bedside of a very wealthy elderly businessman. To say this man had made his mark in the field of corporate investments and takeovers would be an understatement. But he had succeeded at a cost to his family, his social relationships, and his own personal growth. Days away from dying from a heart ailment, he turned to me with a lesson clearly learned too late: "I thought whenever something hurt me I could grit my teeth and show the world who was boss. But it doesn't work that way. It's *who* you love and *how* you love, and the rest of it doesn't mean a thing. Remember that for me, will you?"

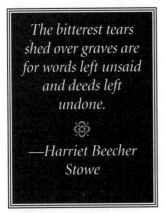

The bitterest tears shed over graves are for words left unsaid and deeds left undone.

—Harriet Beecher Stowe

The gift of this man's dying words has stayed with me through many rough times in my own life. But they did him little good. Had he not gone through life like a rigid warrior, clenching his jaw and fist, waging war against the blows life dealt him, he might have been able to open his heart to the truth, and his arms to his loved ones. The direction in which he could have traveled in life was there to be seen and intuited, but he lacked the vision, or perhaps the time. This business tycoon taught me that, despite his fortune, he was not a success. Sadly, at the end of his days, he was impoverished of spirit and devoid of joy.

But we have chosen another path. We are draining away the *profane* elements of our pain, and discovering the *sacred* within our wounds. We are learning to accept the light of wisdom that emerges out of the darkness of life's challenges. And now we shine the same light upon the pathway that our wounds have revealed. We will come to recognize that far from becoming deadened to life's experiences because of our suffering, our souls are alive! They react and grow. And when our souls grow, our spirit soars.

"It's *who* you love and *how* you love," the businessman observed. And the "who" and "how" begin with ourselves. The past is past. We must not dwell there. We must inhabit the present, as the koan of Joshu tells us. The direction we must take is in the here and now. The gifts of wisdom born of pain and the realization of the precious path we are to follow are capable of enriching our spirits and placing joy in our hearts, two elements that are integral to my definition of success.

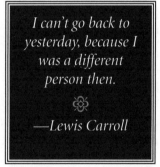

I can't go back to yesterday, because I was a different person then.

—Lewis Carroll

"To love another, one must first love oneself" may be a cliché, but that doesn't make it any less true. When we recognize and claim the journey that is now ours to make because of our wounds, we also recognize that we have *earned* the gift of this precious path. This journey of hope and transformation is our *life-right*. One part of the *Fifth Step* is recognizing that loving oneself means embracing the road signs that a Sacred Wound posts at the start of our quest. A Sacred Wound reminds us, often when we are most vulnerable, that we are eminently deserving of compassion, purpose, and growth.

THE PRECIOUS PATH REVEALED

One signpost we may recognize after having been wounded is that our illusion of the "perfect life" must end. Many of us grow up with the idea that everything will unfold in an orderly and joyous fashion. We will enjoy a childhood filled with youthful celebration, toys and games, birthday parties, and family vacations. As we move toward adulthood, we may keep up a false vision of an idealized existence in which we will fall in love, have our own terrific kids, find a fulfilling job with a boatload of benefits, and make great money. Our lives and those we love will be kissed with health and harmony.

> *Your vision will become clear only when you look into your heart. Who looks outside, dreams. Who looks inside, awakens.*
>
> ⚛
>
> —*Carl Jung*

You might be thinking that anyone who has experienced even a bit of life and still believes such a perfect life is possible is living in an alternative universe. But many of us bought such a vision at one time and nurtured it despite signals to the contrary. And, more to the point, despite knowing that perfection and a painless life are not reality (or even desirable), we will often believe that because of our inability to attain this false vision, we are failures.

As we live and love and lose and learn, however, our hurt and heartache reveal the truth to us. This world we've concocted, with the help of storybooks and celluloid fantasies, is an *illusion*. It doesn't exist. We may fight it. We may even continue to inflict pain on ourselves for some perceived inner disability that has kept us from claiming the prize of these expectations. It is ultimately our wounds—life's harsh imperfections—that help us see things as they truly are. Attaining the success we crave in our personal or professional lives is nearly impossible when we dwell in the world of illusions and false expectations. If we are to survive and succeed in our imperfect lives and our imperfect world, *clarity* is one of the greatest gifts we can receive in helping us to claim our journey.

Another signpost at the start of our precious path comes in relation to our specific pain—our actual loss or injury to body, heart, and/or soul. We might respond to the experience of our trauma by gasping to others and ourselves: *I'll never make it . . . This is too much to bear . . . I'm a weak person. . . .* We might believe we will never again feel joy, know laughter, catch our breath in excitement. We become numb to life. Then, at some point, with the help of a therapist or friend or on our own, we find that we have opened our eyes in the morning and—guess what? We have made it. We're still here, with some pain perhaps, but we've survived. We might find ourselves smiling at someone or moved by a child's playful banter, laughing out loud, *feeling* again. We have come to recognize a voice within our singed souls, speaking to us in the language of awareness, which draws out yet another gift that helps bestow an even deeper appreciation for the simplicity of a budding tree, the joy of a person's touch, the miracle of a new day.

Of all the signs our wounds can post as we embark on our precious path, the most important is the direction to live in the present. For success and transformation cannot simply materialize out of ethereal dreams for the future, they only come into being when we actively *walk the walk in the here and now.*

Having been wounded, we may naturally project all kinds of frightening scenarios about our future. Suddenly, nothing's for sure. We may spin a web of questions: *What if I never love again? What if my child dies? What if I don't get well? What if I stay addicted? What if I don't get this job or raise or promotion?* The future intimidates us. We become lost in a psychological trap of our own making, and can even be in danger of yielding to our self-fulfilling prophecies. But this *profane* message is trumped when we know *how* to listen to the *sacred* in our wounds. Attuning our inner ears to the voice of our painful experiences, we find that if we seek the enlightenment of hope and healing, we must stay grounded in the present and not dwell in the past or fear the future. This is the step we take now—to claim the journey that is ours to make, to find the precious path, and then, equipped with wisdom and the signposts of our wounds, to walk the walk.

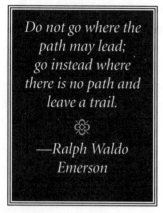

Do not go where the path may lead; go instead where there is no path and leave a trail.

—Ralph Waldo Emerson

Kahlil Gibran said, "Your pain is the breaking of the shell that encloses your understanding." In breaking that shell, we will be able to see that our new direction is a gift received from our Sacred Wounds. Along this precious path of *Step Five,* moving ever closer to empowerment, we find that our quest toward a fuller realization of who we are awaits us. We have only to step forward down the pathway of growth and transformation.

———

Here is the story of a young man who learned about the path that would most affirm all of his dreams by way of his wounds and by embarking on a stunning odyssey. His quest for health took him from the heights of youthful exuberance to a life-threatening disease to a miracle of redemption that defied medical opinion. His journey took him, his family, and doctors into uncharted territory. More than anything, his story exemplifies how gifts born of pain can inspire the triumph of the human spirit.

Steve's Story

*I*t was late afternoon when the message was handed to me in the middle of my class on social action and ethical behavior. While parrying the adolescent outbursts of my high school classroom, I opened the folded note. It read: "Please bring Steven outside now. Don't make it an issue. You will need to join him."

It took a second for the enigmatic message to register. It was vague and alarming at the same time. I tried my best to act nonchalant, asking Steve, one of my students, to give me a hand with some class materials. The director of education met us in the corridor. He pulled me aside, whispering that someone needed to see me and he would keep Steve company until I was done.

Stepping out into the coolness of the approaching evening, I was met by Steve's parents, Dotty and Larry. The look on their faces worried me immediately. A few weeks earlier, they explained, Steve had been complaining of pain around his ribs. He had had it checked out, and it appeared to be nothing. That morning, however, another set of tests came back with a terrifying preliminary finding. It was believed that Steve had a cancerous tumor growing along one of his ribs. He would need to enter the hospital immediately for conclusive tests, but the doctors were not encouraging. Dotty and Larry asked for my help in telling Steve the bad news, and getting him into the car and over to the hospital.

When we came into the quiet school lobby to speak to Steve, the sight of his parents caught him by surprise. Instinctively, he began backing away. I remember seeing his knees buckling a little as we told him the frightening news. Then the protests erupted. Dotty and Larry braced one another while their spirited and frightened firstborn child ranted: "This is a mistake. There's nothing wrong. We don't have to do this, you hear me?!"

Steve was still certain it was all a mistake when we finally checked him into the nearby hospital. The family paced in the corridors while the medical staff settled Steve in his room. We were all awaiting the arrival of a noted oncologist, who had been inundated with requests from family friends that he examine Steve personally.

When the doctor arrived, he was immediately surrounded by

the growing entourage of concerned family members and friends who were urging him to take this boy's case. He explained that he no longer accepted adolescent patients, but having been moved by the flood of phone calls, he would take part in confirming or disputing the diagnosis. I learned later that this sensitive and compassionate man, Dr. Avrum Bluming, had been devastated by the loss of his young cancer patients and that the toll of these emotional wounds cut too deep for him to continue.

Suddenly, the small crowd parted and into the inner circle came Steve's maternal grandmother. She faced the doctor with a look of quiet urgency. She stared into his eyes a moment and then did something I will never forget. Reaching out, she took the oncologist's hands, holding them softly between her own. Looking up with the tenacious glow of love that only a grandparent can produce, she spoke words that blessed the moment with her pain.

"My good doctor . . . I did not escape the horrors of the Siberian labor camps with my husband and my little daughter, Dotty, and walk, near starvation, across Asia so that I could come to this great country and watch my grandson die of cancer. Please," she whispered, her face burnished with tears and hope, "you make him well for me. These hands I am holding have a purpose."

And with that she kissed his hands and softly placed her cheek against them. All who witnessed this sacred moment were impacted by the power of the human heart to transform another's mission. (And it would not be the last time a single soul would change the course of events in the quest to keep Steve alive.) The stunned doctor stared into the older woman's eyes. Gathering a deep breath, he nodded slowly and asked for Steve's room.

I was asked to join Dr. Bluming as a nonfamily member whom Steve trusted. The oncologist explained that we would need to convince Steve to undergo a procedure to verify the cancer diagnosis. With young people, he told me, it was not always an easy decision. I would soon find out why. After sharing a few words and trying to calm a very frightened young man, Dr. Bluming prevailed on Steve to go through with the test so we could all know with certainty what he was facing. Steve, rebelling against this invasion into his life, nevertheless warmed to the idea of disproving the original diagnosis. As his initial resistance showed signs of crumbling, Dr. Bluming called on the nurse, who immediately produced a very long needle with a tiny pincer on the end. Steve's eyes opened wide in alarm. The doctor gently encouraged him, promising that he just needed to nudge it into his hip and take a tiny bone chip. Steve studied his face, then looked over at mine. Taking a deep breath, he clenched his jaw and nodded.

I've never seen anyone spring into action as quickly as Dr. Bluming. Before Steve could change his mind, the oncologist had turned him on his side, prepped the area around his hip, inserted the mammoth needle, and twisted it in one single fluid motion. There was a small but perceptible *snap*, and then he swiftly withdrew the instrument with a huge grin. It was over. Steve, drenched in sweat, slumped over in relief. The doctor placed his hand on Steven's. "You did great," he assured him. Steve smiled weakly, and promptly passed out.

The diagnosis confirmed everyone's deepest fears. Steve had a cancer identified as Ewing's sarcoma, a small round-cell cancer that usually strikes children between the ages of ten and twenty. It is considered to be the most lethal of all bone tumors. The survival rates have greatly improved, but twenty-two years ago, at the time Steve's case was diagnosed, he was given a 10 to 15 percent chance of living beyond a few years. His family, which included his younger twin brothers, Scott and Kenny, was shaken to its foundations. But they were all resolute. Steve was a fighter. They were fighters, too. Somehow they would beat this thing together.

Dr. Bluming then told the family more shocking news—the surgeons recognized that the standard course of action would be to carve the tumor and surrounding areas directly out of his chest. This surgery would leave Steve in a precarious physical condition—not to mention what it would do to the mental state of a proud young man suddenly finding himself physically disfigured—and it was possible that Steve would die of this "cure." Instead, Dr. Bluming decided to put Steve through the then inexact regimen of chemotherapy. The idea was to shrink the tumor enough that its removal would not require a radical amputation of portions of his upper body. But the medical profession was unsure about the correct calibration of chemicals, and even less certain about how well Steve would weather the dangerous side effects they could produce. With all of this roiling in the minds of doctor, patient, family, and friends, the quest to save Steve began.

Steve tried his best to put on a good face for everyone. Always mischievous, he soon became a favorite of the nurses, even after his friends got caught trying to smuggle a six-foot submarine sandwich into the hospital. Flashing his trademark grin, he also endeared himself to the doctors and support staff who were helping him through the chemo treatments.

The procedure was a living hell. After each treatment, Steve would go home, where his young brothers would hear him vomiting violently. Dotty would wait until he was asleep before picking up his clothes and removing the hairs that had fallen from his head, to spare him from seeing his loss first thing in the morning. She would wash and redrape the clothes exactly as Steven had left them; she would then retire to the bathroom, where she would curl up on the floor and sob into the carpet.

In between the harsh chemotherapy treatments, the family tried to live life as normally as possible. Every once in a while, when they least expected it, they were even able to find humor. One day, they were all gathered in the living room watching a football game. Suddenly, a commercial came on for a hair product for men. A beautiful woman was shown running her fingers through the rich, thick hair of her male companion, urging the audience to use the "shampoo that makes the most of what you've got." The room collectively held its breath as everyone avoided looking at Steve. The twins each stole a glance, Dotty hid her eyes, Larry shifted uncomfortably. Suddenly, the silence was punctured by Steve's generous laughter. And then the whole family was joining in, laughing uncontrollably at everything they couldn't control. Warmth and love and sadness were all bound up in the laughter between the tears.

Over the next few months, Steve would lose all of his hair. He began wearing a wig designed to match his usual style. Steve did his best to maintain his self-image as a cool guy and a heart-breaker. He had managed to keep his condition secret from everyone but his closest friends. One night, at the end of a terrific date, his girlfriend turned to him and planted a hot kiss right on his lips. Tugging playfully at his hair, she kissed him again and again, until suddenly his hair was moving, sliding across his scalp. Backing away, she screamed, "What is that? My God, it's not even your own hair!" Steve straightened the wig and fired back, "You bet it is. I paid good money for it!" It was classic Steve: even in the throes of pain, he had a feisty pride I couldn't help but admire.

But as time progressed and the chemo took its toll, Steve got less and less willing to go through it all. He felt it was killing him, and in a sense it was: the chemicals attack good cells as well as cancer cells. In addition to his hair, he had been losing stamina, and began openly asking why he should put himself through it. Steve was at the breaking point. Joseph Campbell would call this moment the "road of trials" that punctuates every heroic quest. But this road showed no prospect of ending.

Even in his pain and anger, however, Steve was facing a kind of enlightenment, discovering a consciousness he had never before possessed. He became acutely aware of the subtle negative messages he and his fellow cancer patients were receiving, which telegraphed defeat rather than hope. When he was hospitalized for additional tests, he listened as medical personnel gossiped insensitively about a poor prognosis in front of older patients, talking about them as if they weren't there. He knew there were some very caring people working in the unit. He had met them. But what was it with the rest of these people? Couldn't they see that these patients had feelings? And the facility itself was depressing—antiseptic and dull. After one particular blowup, during which he had once again tried to smuggle in what he called "human food," Steve lost it.

It was in this vulnerable condition that he first heard a voice rise from deep within him. It was the voice of his pain, demanding dignity. He was growing as a man even as he faced his greatest danger—his own death.

Flashing anger and desperation, Steve confronted a line of caregivers with nothing less than a declaration of rights: "We're not dead. You got that? Those of us with cancer, with all these tubes and disgusting chemo treatments—we're not dead. You freakin' people give us gray walls, gray food. How do you expect people to get better when you've already put us in the goddamn morgue?!" The attendants and nurses were taken aback. Although some were angry about being lectured by a rule-breaking kid, others would say later that they were moved profoundly by this gift of insight from someone so young.

Steve's journey toward health continued on its rocky path. One day, he bolted from the hospital just before his treatment. He felt as if his whole world were a stinging wound, and in the quest to save his own life he was being poisoned again and again by nausea, exhaustion, and his inability to enjoy life on his own terms. His father finally managed to corner Steve and urge him to come back to the hospital. Steve, eyes searching for an escape route, finally leaped atop a fence, screaming back that if his father came any closer he would "f———kin' kill myself."

Nearly breathless and doubled over, Larry managed to look up at his son and speak what was in his heart: "You can run from me,

Steven, but you can't run away from yourself. I know you're angry at what's inside you, but you've got to . . ." At that moment, as Steve straddled the fence, a pair of attack dogs came leaping and snarling at him from the other side. In an instant, Steve had jumped back into the safety of his father's arms.

Later at the hospital, Dr. Bluming and I were alone with Steve, trying to persuade him to take his treatment. We went over and over the importance of the chemotherapy. We each expressed empathy for what he was going through, but also stressed the consequences of stopping midway through the regimen. Steve didn't want to hear it. Finally, a monumental silence settled in the room. The doctor and I exchanged glances, wondering what to do next. I struggled to find the right words, something that would not only arouse Steve's sense of physical survival but his fighting spirit as well. After a moment, however, it was this compassionate and well-versed oncologist who did it for both of us.

Dr. Bluming turned to Steve, who sat between us in a darkened room off the lobby of the hospital, and spoke softly. "Steven, I can't begin to know your pain, and I've seen more of this kind of suffering than most. But I believe there is a gift here. If you'll face what has happened to you and let me help you, there's an opportunity for you to do something. The Talmud says that whosoever saves one life, it is counted as if he saved the entire world. Someone out there needs you. I don't know how or when. Let me try to help you so that *you* can save another life, another world." Steve looked up and stared at the doctor, a mixture of pain and shock crossing his face. Then, quietly, he said, "Okay. Let's do it."

Steve was on a path that seemed to twist and turn with the hills and valleys of hope and despair, and along the way he was forced to do continuous battle with inner demons, the messages from the tumor within him that whispered that it was all too much to bear. At other times, though, he would hear another voice springing from his pain, encouraging him to hold on, telling him that there was light to be seen in the struggle to survive. It's what led him into a church one day, after being shaken up by a TV evangelist's warning to "repent before Christ returns." Steve had had his bar mitzvah a few years earlier, but in his vulnerable state, on a journey fraught with fear and peril, he was searching for comfort.

He sat for a while on a pew inside the church, taking in all the unfamiliar statues and symbols, until an elderly priest approached him. "Can I help you, my son?" Steve was nervous; suddenly he had no idea what he was doing there. Finally he managed to stammer: "Look, I'm a Jew, all right, but I've got this tumor inside me and I might die, so I thought—well, what if you guys are right?" The old priest smiled and sat down next to Steve. Patting him on the shoulder, he assured him, "We don't have anything here that you don't already have in your faith, my son. There is great strength in your tradition. You can find what you're looking for there, this I know." And then he offered a prayer for Steve and wished him peace. Later, back at home, Steve managed to laugh at his one-on-one in the church. Cancer is one strange trip, he thought; you never know where it's going to take you.

As the nausea continued to rack his body after each chemo treatment, Dotty and Larry asked Dr. Bluming for something that might lessen its impact. They were informed that one of the best ways to treat the nausea wasn't legal, but if they could somehow manage to procure a little of it, it would certainly help. This is how a fairly conservative middle-class mom found herself on a street corner in Santa Monica scoring a bag of weed. Later at home, she took the bag and the papers into Steve's bedroom as he lay shivering after a bout of vomiting. Taking out the marijuana and papers, she began wrestling awkwardly with the task of rolling a joint. She was becoming increasingly frustrated when Steve looked up and, dumbfounded, realized what his mom was doing. Unable to bear her fumbling, he took the papers and bag of marijuana from her and rolled a perfect joint in a matter of seconds. Dotty tried not to look impressed. He told her he thought he'd died and gone to heaven—his own mom was actually helping him get high. The cancer had produced a lot of agony. But it also produced an incredible closeness between mother and son, a gift emerging from their shared quest for Steve's survival. It was a feeling they would both treasure and draw upon in the days ahead.

One afternoon, Steve had just returned home from his ninth treatment when, almost immediately, Dotty heard a crash from his bedroom. Throwing open the door she found him convulsing on the floor in a violent reaction to the chemotherapy. Gathering him up as fast as she could, she half-carried, half-dragged him to the car. Tearing out of the driveway, Dotty cradled Steve's shaking body with one arm as she raced the car through stop signs all the way to Dr. Bluming's offices next to the hospital. The doctors' parking entrance was closest, but the barrier arm blocked her path. Honking wildly, she shouted at the guard to open it up for an emergency. He approached, telling her calmly to go around the block to the patients' entrance. In a flash, Dotty backed up the car a few feet and to the astonishment of the guard, flipped it into drive and rammed the car straight through the barrier arm and into the parking garage.

When people face danger, there is an adrenaline rush that gives them superhuman strength. Mothers have been known to lift up the front end of a car in order to free children pinned beneath. Dotty possessed that same kind of strength at this moment. Gasping, she pulled her convulsing full-grown son into her arms and onto the elevator. When the door opened onto the oncologist's office, she burst into a doctors' meeting, laying Steven on the table with the demand "Save my son." As Dr. Bluming's colleague and a nurse took over, he tried to calm Dotty down, explaining to her that Steve was having a reaction to the chemotherapy and that he would be all right.

Then the oncologist turned grim. "Dotty," he said, "I know this is going to be rough to hear, but the tumor isn't shrinking.

We've all decided that we shouldn't put Steven through this any-more. This is simply killing him. We're going to stop treatment." Dotty took a step back. "You're quitting?" Dr. Bluming insisted there was nothing more to do. They could try radical surgery, but it didn't look promising. There was no point torturing his body with chemotherapy if it wasn't working. But Dotty wasn't having any of it. "Look at me. *I'll* tell you when you're finished working on Steven. It's not over. Do you hear me? It's not over. We're going to *save my son*." Bluming studied her for a moment and began trying to convince her again, but then he lapsed into silence. In the same way Steve had answered Dr. Bluming's own plea to help save a single life, he said softly, "Okay. We'll keep going."

Faced with so grave a threat to her child's life, Dotty was dis-covering within herself a strength and a voice she had never known before. She and Larry were companions on this quest for survival. They, too, were suffering wounds—wounds made *sacred* by an inner voice demanding they take a vigilant, unceasing role in saving their son.

Three weeks after these events, and two months before the end of his regimen, a friend of Steve's dropped off a letter he had written to his parents. Larry and Dotty had recently granted Steve's wish to have a measure of freedom by moving him into a summer apartment near their home. He would be preparing for college soon, and he wanted to feel what it would be like to have his own space. After watching him suffer through so much of the last year, still uncertain of what the future would bring, his par-ents decided to go along. In the letter, Steve informed them that he was going to drive up the coast of California for a little get-away before his final two treatments. He insisted he just needed a little breathing room before facing the upcoming challenge of the procedures. He knew they would have tried to talk him out of it, he wrote, so he decided to put it in a letter. Worried and agitated, Larry and Dotty decided to try to take it in stride. They realized that throughout the summer, Steve was attempting to take back a little control over his own life. They would have to trust him.

Realizing that Steve would have to vacate his summer-lease apartment upon his return, Larry decided to help by moving him out. Steve would have enough to handle when he returned from his trip. While packing up Steve's dresser, he came upon a document that baffled him. It was a receipt made out to a Steven Barth. Why would Steve have this other guy's papers, Larry wondered? As he examined the receipt more closely, he realized that it was for a plane ticket . . . to Hawaii. One-way. Larry checked the date. It was for *that day*. And as the truth dawned on him, it was like a kick to the heart—Steve wasn't going up the coast for a couple of weeks. He was going to Hawaii. And he wasn't planning on coming back.

After interviewing some of Steve's friends and his therapist, Larry and Dotty quickly put together the picture. The truth, they learned, was that the minimal progress, the percentages stacked against him, the prospect he might still have to have big parts of his chest amputated, and the looming possibility that the cancer cells had already migrated, had convinced Steve that his life was over. None of his friends thought he'd run away, but they knew he was in a bad place. The Hawaii destination, however, was a surprise to everyone. He had always wanted to visit the islands, and now he was going there to die.

There had always been one given in this entire quest to save Steve's life—he could not afford to miss a single treatment. Contacting the Hawaii police, the airport, and the airline, Larry finally persuaded everyone that the kid on that plane was flying under an alias. He was going to Hawaii and would die without treatment. They had to bring him back.

When Steve landed in Honolulu, he was stunned to hear "Steven Brody" being paged over the loudspeakers as he walked through the terminal. Panicking, he began to run. He had been through so many obstacles on his journey of pain; all he wanted now was to be left alone. What did the world have against him that he couldn't just disappear and face what time he had left without hassles? The wounds within his body and mind were on fire, burning away any vision of hope. His quest to survive, he had determined, was over. And now there were even roadblocks to the end of his road! When the airport police recognized Steve, and gave chase, Steve panicked. Refusing to slow down, he jumped a barrier and raced up a down escalator. Barely eluding the grasp of one of the officers, he searched for a way out. Catching sight of an exit less than a hundred feet away, Steve ducked under a railing, threw back a luggage cart in the direction of his pursuers, and sprinted toward his escape. Out of nowhere, an enforcement stick flew across the floor at his feet. Ten yards away from slipping their grasp, Steve went tumbling to the ground. In a flash, the officers had him. Bruised and baffled as to how it had all gone wrong, he was escorted to the next available flight back to L.A. He couldn't know then that the refusal of his parents to give up—their determination to intercept him even on an island in the Pacific—would have profound consequences in restoring his quest for life.

Back at Los Angeles Airport, Steve's family waited as he came off the plane. Tears brimmed in his grandmother's eyes as she and his other grandparents hugged him first. His brothers wrapped their arms around his waist as he looked into the faces of his parents. Then the clouds burst open, and Steve felt the love around him drowning out his despair. He had tried to run from everyone he loved. His pain and the fear it engendered were trying to remove him from life. Giving up wasn't the answer. Suddenly, he became aware of a voice within his pain sending out a different message. If his pain could inspire those he loved to fight this hard for his life, then he could, too. Recognizing that a new pathway to his goal awaited him transformed his outlook, and Steve gave himself over once more to his journey for survival without further protest.

The news following the very next chemotherapy treatment was cautiously but definitely encouraging. Miraculously, there was a noticeable shrinking of the tumor. Dr. Bluming had been recalibrating the chemotherapy drugs constantly, and to his amazement and delight he'd finally hit upon a promising combination. After one more treatment, they would be ready to go in and find out if the tumor could be removed completely, and whether or not the cancer had spread.

On the day of the surgery there was a small village camped out in the hospital corridors. Steve's grandmother blessed her grandson. Steve told his younger brothers it was going to be all right and trembled as his parents kissed him; then, with a thumbs-up, he bravely headed to surgery on the wheels of hope. The surgery took four and a half hours. When Dr. Bluming emerged, he told Dotty, Larry, and the family that they had removed a single rib with a tumor intact. Astonishingly, it appeared that the cancer had not spread. They would have to wait for the pathology report to verify it, but Dotty and Larry already knew. Their son was going to live. They collapsed into each other's arms as Steve's brothers held on tightly and wept. Steve's grandmother held Bluming's hands once more, and thanked him through her tears for all he had done.

The pathology report gave Steve a clean bill of health. They would have to continue to monitor him, but if he could make it past the seven-year mark, it was highly unlikely that the cancer would ever return.

Steve was seventeen at the time of the surgery. Today, twenty-two years later, he is a recently married man in his late thirties, still sharing his cocky grin and a mischievous nature with family and friends. He and his wife are planning on having a family, and all that came about from choosing the precious path of living for today as the best foundation for achieving his dreams for tomorrow.

Before we leave Steve's story, there is a single incident you will be blessed to know. It occurred on the evening of the day Steve's doctor had convinced him to take his treatment by quoting the Talmud: "He who saves one life saves the entire world." I had been

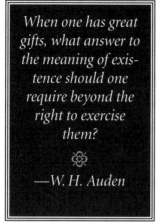

> *When one has great gifts, what answer to the meaning of existence should one require beyond the right to exercise them?*
>
> ❦
>
> —*W. H. Auden*

in the room to witness a doctor teaching this very ill young man that life has many gifts. And among them is our ability, even when we are in pain, to help a fellow human being. Dr. Bluming had told Steve that his life had a purpose, and he had instilled in him, if only for that day, the belief that one person can make a difference. "Let me help save you, Steven," the doctor had said, "so that you can save another."

That night, one of Steve's fellow cancer patients had called him at home. She was giving up and called to let him know she was planning to take her own life that very night. He, of all people, would understand, she said. Although he was recuperating from the day's chemo regimen, nauseated and racked with spasms, Steve managed to keep her talking, and distracted, while he signaled for help on another phone line. Steve was there for her until assistance arrived. He was credited with having saved her life. In so doing, he had preserved a world.

Is there a greater pathway upon which to tread?

———

When we are in the midst of our pain, it is often impossible to recognize the road we must choose. If you are currently going through the throes of disease, divorce, loss of a job or loved one, or some other life-shattering experience, I implore you to *be gentle on yourself*. The direction you are to take may not be readily apparent. You may lose sight of your quest to find meaning in your pain. Your journey to claim your Sacred Wounds may not yet have begun. But know this much—the precious path *will* unfold. If you seek it, you will find it and claim it as your own. Give the journey, and yourself, time.

———

We may be walking through a market, humming a song, preparing dinner, hiking the Grand Canyon, or putting money in a meter, and somehow, incredibly, *that* is the moment when we connect with the universe in the blessing of enlightenment revealed from our wounds. It could be the sudden rush of a deep breath taken in appreciation for the beauty of nature, something we had ignored until the pain of an illness gifted us with awareness. Then again, we might suddenly realize how special it is to have a family for whom we are fixing a meal after mourning the loss of a parent. We may not have recognized this pathway of awareness and appreciation intellectually, but now it is *felt* in the journey we have chosen to live and experience life a day at a time. We may finally intuit the gift of the beauty all around us or the newfound meaning certain people have in our lives: we may *feel* this new path we're on in a sudden rush of hope, the uplift of gratefulness, and when we do, the light of this feeling spreads from the inside out.

I had a moment like this following a devastating breakup. Having dared to love once more, here I was again. The sense of rejection was overwhelming. I was enveloped in sadness and despair, trying madly to figure out what the experience had all meant and whether there could be any goodness to be mined from such pain. An alarm bell was going off in my head telling me that if I didn't physically pick myself up and move on, I would fall into an abyss from which I couldn't climb out. I went back home to Vermont in some hope of finding solace. My mother always had gifts of wisdom for me. But after a few days I felt the need to spend some time alone, and soon found myself driving through my native New England, looking for answers, finding none. All I could feel was a grief and a darkness.

Eventually I made my way to the coast of Maine, and pulled into a small fishing village. Admiring the magnificent vista of the

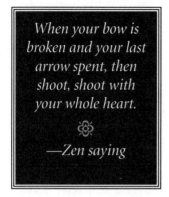

When your bow is broken and your last arrow spent, then shoot, shoot with your whole heart.

—Zen saying

Atlantic, I decided to go out for a walk along the ocean, which was fierce and tempest-tossed, the wind blowing at a maddening clip. After some time, lost in my own fog, I came upon a rock that extended out to sea. I climbed upon it and took in the cloudy skies interspersed with stabbing rays of light.

I don't know how long I stood there, casting my eyes across the expanse of the Atlantic, feeling without relief the gaping wound within me. After some time, however, my attention turned to the large fragment of rock upon which I was standing. It was jutting out into the water, but still grounded firmly on the mainland. On this rocky perch on the edge of America, staring down at the stone surface beneath me, I became aware of the rock's weather-beaten features—its fissures, the scars on its surface. And in a moment I can only describe as full-blown *enlightenment*, I understood that this rock was just like my heart, scarred from my original divorce and now, years later, the loss of yet another so dear to me. And as I felt the spray of the water and the fierce wind batter the rock, this recognition was born as a gift within me. I knew that for all my heart had encountered, it was still here—weathered and imposing. It had incorporated the wounds suffered by exposure to life's elements into its very design and remained strong. My heart was and would be the same.

Lifting my eyes, I looked out at the drama of the ocean, the wind kicking up whitecaps, the sun's rays like brushes of light painting its canvas. This rock didn't know what the universe had in store for it and I didn't know what the future held for me. But I was suddenly filled with the certain knowledge of my own ability to weather what was to come. And I was keenly aware that this new pathway of self-knowledge had sprung fully formed from the wound within me.

———

THE TASK

Recognizing the signposts within our pain allows us to be enlightened by our Sacred Wounds as they reveal the precious path we can travel toward success. These markers of enlightenment, which provide us with tools with which to make this journey, may include: the need to drop our illusions of a perfect life, the recognition that we have the capacity for joy and can embrace it more fully after having been wounded, the ability to see clearly what is meaningful in life, the desire to express appreciation for the wonder all around us, and the importance of living in the present.

Using the signpost-finding tools of the following questions, take time to recognize the signals pointing you to your own path of living in the present. As you contemplate the answers, record them in your journal:

Think about a single wound you have experienced.

- ❀ What in your life became more important as a result of your pain?
- ❀ Are there relationships that have become trivial while others became more starkly essential to your well-being *because* of your pain?
- ❀ Do you notice moments when you feel an appreciation that you never felt before this wound entered your life? For example, do you experience sunsets differently? Or the kindness others show to you? Do you notice how *you* treat others with more clarity? Write about it. Describe a moment when you seemed to have a "new pair of eyes" and how you felt seeing that moment.

❀ Do you appreciate your own gifts for endurance and survival? If you don't, shouldn't you? Think about it. Express what this gift means to you.

❀ What do you know about your quest for success that you didn't know before your spirit was wounded? Have your goals for success changed? Has your definition of success been altered?

Take time to marinate in these questions. They will bring clarity, yes, and enlightenment.

THE RITUAL

Select and decorate a small box. It might be a shoe box, it could be a small wooden one, the kind you can purchase inexpensively in a crafts store. Express who you are by painting, covering with colored paper, or printing something of your unique spirit on this box. It is your box of enlightenment.

Look over all the answers that you've written in your journal and select a few of the enlightened signposts you've received that point you in a new direction. Inscribe them in your own handwriting on small strips of paper or on cards. Read each one before placing them in your box of enlightenment, a keepsake that you will add to every time you come to a new awareness that has evolved out of your wounds.

THE GIFT

The miracles of self-knowledge affirm the enlightened path that our hurtful experiences have helped to create:

❀ The pain I have encountered contains an opportunity for me to see the precious path I wish to take on my quest for success.

❀ If I hold on to the false vision of perfection, I realize it is a certain path to a life of regret.

❀ Living in the present is the only way to build a foundation
  for my dreams of the future.
❀ The gifts of my wounds lift my heart, my mind, my soul.
  They belong to me. I treasure myself when I treasure
  them.
❀ In every experience in life, even the painful ones, there is a
  gift. I can and will find it.

———

Remember the words of the businessman who shared with me
what he had learned from the pain of his life as he lay dying: "It's
who you love and *how* you love." The
rest, as he pointed out, doesn't mean a
thing in the grand scheme of our lives.

Recognizing and claiming the journey that is ours alone to make is also
our way of affirming that the *who* and
how of loving begins with the experience of loving ourselves. It is a precious path that can only be discovered
by way of our wounds.

Claiming our Sacred Wounds and

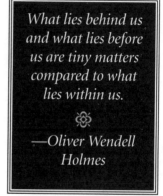

*What lies behind us
and what lies before
us are tiny matters
compared to what
lies within us.*

❀

*—Oliver Wendell
Holmes*

using them to empower us toward achieving the success we want
is an act of self-love. Knowing that we deserve that love and that
success is a precious gift of enlightenment that our soul is waiting
to bestow.

Step Five has led us to recognize the signposts and to claim the
route we must now take, a route revealed by our wounds. It now
delivers us to *Step Six,* where we will allow ourselves to honor our
wounds by following our new awareness as it propels us toward
assisting others along our way. It is through this step of *purposeful living* that we claim the *sacred* gift of meaning so necessary to
the precious path of our success.

STEP SIX

HONORING THE WOUND: The Bridge to Purposeful Living

Action is eloquence.
—William Shakespeare

THE MEDITATION

I am the sum of my parts
and so much more—
physical, emotional, spiritual,
my hopes, my dreams and . . .
aspects I have yet to discover.

I treasure what I know, and
what I may yet uncover.

I honor the many facets
of who I am.
The hurt I've experienced,
my ability to heal.
My capacity to spread that healing,
and find purpose in the pain.
Let me sit for a while

in the light of my being,
cradling my spirit
and the tenderness of my wounds;
paying tribute to their existence—
for they are part of what makes me *who* I am.

———

The Talmud makes the following poetic affirmation:

Every blade of grass has its angel
that bends over it and whispers,
grow, grow.

We might wish for the very same treatment and wonder if there will ever be an "angel" by our side telling us to "*Grow, grow.*" We may have been at the end of our tether any number of times. Wouldn't it have been nice to have that angel, our own personal trainer of the spirit, to urge us ever forward? Yet as we've learned over the last *five steps*, having been wounded does not diminish or destroy us, for we are still here. And even more significantly—we can still *grow.*

Perhaps there *are* angels whispering in our ears and in our hearts after all.

To become empowered by the pain we have endured, we have begun by taking the necessary *steps.* First, in *Step One,* we acknowledged our wounds, accessing the consciousness that comes with opening our awareness. Next, in *Step Two,* we began letting go of the guilt associated with this pain, removing the barriers to entering the kingdom of healing by recognizing the cost of self-blame and guilt. We then exam-

> *It is one of the most beautiful compensations of this life that no man can sincerely try to help another without helping himself.*
>
> ✿
>
> —Ralph Waldo Emerson

ined our *core beliefs* in *Step Three,* draining away the *profane* elements that obscure the *sacred* light from which we might draw illumination and positive energy. In *Step Four,* we learned to accept the wisdom that brings forth newfound insights with which we can move toward success. And in *Step Five,* we claimed our journey of clarity, the precious path of living in the present that can lead us to all we want to be. Now, in *Step Six,* we will learn to honor the pain we have experienced, and deepen the journey we have chosen, by heeding the call from within our wounds that urges us to respond to the pain of others.

PAIN WITH PURPOSE

*W*hen we can reach out to bring about healing in someone else's life, we honor the enlightened path of our own wounds that we discovered in the *Fifth Step.* Why? Because by being consciously aware that our compassion has been reawakened by our wounded spirit, *we sanctify our pain with purpose.*

The friend who spent the night with us in the aftermath of our father's death, the husband who came with us to every chemotherapy appointment, the stranger who noticed our tears over our son's drug problem and stopped to comfort us. All of these people have shown empathy and compassion in responding to our pain. We honor our wounds, and the acts of these "angels" who have encouraged us to grow, by purposefully placing empathy out into the world.

When our wounds cause us not only to hear the pain of a family member, friend, or stranger, but to respond, we elevate our own experience of suffering. This bridge to *purposeful living—* empathy, care, and community—is a key element of *Step Six.* Using our pain to produce it is part of the way we honor the experience of our life's wounds. Honoring the wounds of others is a key to living a life of meaning. In the Jewish tradition, there is a powerful myth that says that in every generation, there are thirty-six righteous individuals, the *lamed vavniks*, for whose sake the world is sustained. The individuals themselves are unaware that they are part of this honored group; they could be any of us. We may glimpse them in their acts of compassion, for their acts of *caring* set them apart. Another pathway of compassion is that of the *bodhisattvas* in Mahayana Buddhism. A bodhisattva is someone who has chosen to attain enlightenment not so he or she can be rewarded with the gift of Nirvana, but rather to aid others to find release from their pain. It is in bringing assistance to those in need that the bodhisattva honors the path of his or her own enlightenment.

In turning our wisdom and the enlightened journey we have claimed from our wounds outward into the world, we embody compassion and the power of the *sacred* within our pain to touch others. Successful living is *purposeful living*. The path of clarity and appreciation we derive from our suffering, as we learned in *Step Five*, allows us to recognize the part and purpose we can play in the entire circle of life. *Step Six* leads us further along our quest, propelling us to step into that role. Seeing and hearing the pain of others is one matter, but taking action elevates the *sacred* within us to a whole new level. And the thing about being raised to a higher level of consciousness is that it enables us to *see so much more*. This increased vision is integral to our growth and success. This vision can provide us with a bridge to others that leads us away from self-indulgent and egocentric behavior, away from getting caught up in our own pain. When there is no bridge to others, we become an island unto ourselves. Upon such solitary territory, success can have little meaning and life can have little purpose. Honoring our wounds, therefore, is the bridge to *purposeful living*.

LIFE IS A WATER WHEEL

*H*ow we connect our Sacred Wounds to the world around us has a lot to do with the compassion this pain calls up in us. In *Step Six* we come to see that our responses to others in need are like a stone dropped into the water, sending out a ripple effect in concentric circles, extending our influence beyond what we thought possible. Such an act we find in the following parable:

There was a miller living by a river, a good distance from his countrymen. He had suffered the loss of his beloved wife several years earlier, but felt that by continuing to fulfill his duties and living the life they had cherished by the water, he was honoring her memory. So once a month he would come to town, sell his bags of wheat, enjoy a single tankard of ale at the local inn, and return home. On one such occasion, the miller chanced upon a farmer and his horse en route to town. The farmer was sitting by the side of the road; and as best the miller could tell, he'd been there for quite some time. He was in deep distress because his horse had come up lame. There was no way he would make it to market with the injured animal, and therefore he wouldn't be able to sell his milk. The miller then offered to help, but the two men could not move the horse. The miller then thought that perhaps he could sell the milk for the farmer, but there was simply no room on his own cart, which was already straining with bags of milled wheat. The farmer thanked the miller and urged him not to be tardy to market because of his misfortune. With some parting words of sympathy, the miller bade the farmer farewell and hurried to take up his post in the town market.

When the miller completed selling his wheat that day, he went for his traditional tankard of ale. Remembering that the farmer was at the side of the road with an injured animal, and that the man had lost his wages for the milk he couldn't sell, the miller changed his plan. Purchasing provisions for a good supper, he made haste back toward the farmer, arriving just as the sun was setting. The farmer, still deep in misery, was surprised and moved. True, the gesture and good food would not replace the loss of his income. And of course his horse was still lame. But he was surely fortunate to have met up with such bountiful and stirring compassion, and the food and company helped him bear his losses.

When he asked the miller why he deserved the honor of this kindness, the miller shook his head. "You have it wrong, my good man," he replied. "The honor was in the giving." "But I wish to repay you," insisted the farmer. The miller thought about it and finally said, "Then remember our meeting as part of what you will say about this difficult day." But the farmer shook his head. "Sir, you are too kind. You took time from your own business on two occasions today; you brought me food and helped lift my spirits. And all this for someone you've never met." The miller smiled and said, "But my friend, I also sought to help you for the person you will help down the road—and for *his* livestock and *his* family. And the people he and his children will help after that. Life is like the water wheel that helps me grind my grain. It all moves in a circle."

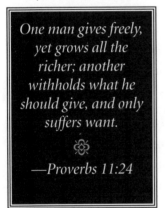

> One man gives freely, yet grows all the richer; another withholds what he should give, and only suffers want.
>
> —Proverbs 11:24

The miller asked the farmer to change the manner in which his unfortunate journey would be remembered. He wanted him to see the way a single person can transform another who is in pain. The miller wanted the farmer to know that repaying someone for kindness shown in time of misfortune was not necessary; it was not a quid pro quo proposition. Rather, he hoped that the farmer would be inspired to help others in their time of distress because he had been helped. Thus the farmer would honor not only the miller's actions but also the pain he himself had experienced.

USING HONOR TO BROADEN OUR SUCCESS

Of course, some people misappropriate the use of honor when it comes to the pain they've endured. Some use their wound as a badge of self-pity, believing that discussing the painful experience in all kinds of public settings is somehow paying tribute to their own suffering. But making a public spectacle of our wound by talking incessantly about it does not invest our pain with purpose; rather, it *steals sacredness from the experience.*

I knew a man who would bring up his wife's death at every occasion he could. It is one thing to speak about it in a support group or with close friends. But this gentleman would launch into how much he had suffered in the middle of parent-teacher conferences and school socials. His story was delivered almost as a reprimand of sorts. He seemed to be bragging about his pain, using a self-righteous tone that suggested that his listeners didn't understand what was important in life. Most saw him as a broken individual who was using his pain as a substitute for getting on with his life. Clearly, the *core belief* tied to his wound had given him the *profane* message that his worth was tied solely to how much he had suffered.

Honoring our wounds also involves taking a step to broaden our understanding of the success we have already achieved *because* of our wounds. We succeed when we acknowledge our pain, dismantle the architecture of self-blame and *profane* suffering, and accept the wisdom our wounds provide us. And most emphatically we succeed when the wound within us elevates our empathy and compassion. In other words, we succeed when our *definition* of success is transformed and redirected by our new vision of the *sacred* qualities of our wounded self. The mapping out of this new direction of honor makes manifest another *sacred* element of our wounds: their ability to create *more* humanity within us, not less.

For some, the *profane* within their pain leads them far away from others, into isolation and increased pain. Sacred Wounds lead us in the opposite direction. Using our pain to increase our consciousness of others enhances our spirit. Using it to deepen our compassion broadens who we are and brings clarity to who we *can* be. Walking the walk of empathy, care, and community transforms our ability to succeed by drawing us back into the circle of life, engaging us in the human endeavor of making a difference not only in our own lives but in the lives of others. We find that we are able to hear and help heal the wounds of our fellow travelers because of our own wounds. In doing so, we send out circles of compassion and blessing that will touch the community, and create within us the motivating message—our success can be deeper, broader, and richer because *our pain has shown us purpose.*

————

I want to tell you the story of a man who has touched my life by the way in which he embraced and honored his wounds, against all odds. He is a man who honors his suffering by putting healing back into the world through creativity and humanity. You will see that he not only hears the voices of the human "angels" who whisper "*Grow, grow!*" but that he, in turn, even *became* an angel for the children of those who wounded him.

Kurt's Story

*T*he turbulent world of the 1930s and early 1940s is the backdrop for Kurt Bronner's coming of age—and a more perilous passage through adolescence would be difficult to imagine.

Kurt was a child of Budapest, Hungary. As a Jew growing up during the rise of Nazi power, his family and friendships were extremely precious. As pressure increased in his country and city to capitulate to the Germans, whose menacing influence was growing rapidly in Hungary, the only thing Kurt could truly count on was the faith that his neighbors would protect him, his family, and their property in times of need.

The city of Budapest is actually made up of what were once two cities—Buda and Pest, separated by the Danube River. Kurt's neighborhood was on the Buda side, home of the Buda Royal Castle and other symbols of Hungary's former glory. Kurt was an only child, "the spoiled center," he says, of his father, Ervin, and his mother, Zelma. His family lived in the area known as the Hill of the Roses. Growing up, he played like every other child among the neighborhood children, and his family was fully integrated into Hungarian life. But with the growth of the Third Reich, the divisiveness and grim reality of hatred began to creep into Kurt's world. When he was seventeen years old, he was ripped from his family and drafted into a Hungarian Labor Brigade. Taken from his beloved Hill of the Roses, Kurt was forced into harsh working conditions in the Transylvanian countryside. There, wearing the yellow armband identifying him as a Jew, Kurt tasted cruelty in the ugly guise of "patriotism." Nevertheless, he held to the dream that this nightmare would somehow pass and that he would soon be reunited with his family on the Hill of the Roses in a Budapest that had been restored to its senses.

After several months in forced-labor conditions, Kurt and some of his fellow workers managed to pool what money they had in order to pay off the soldiers who were finishing their tenure in the battalion. Rather than be sent off to another front or labor camp, Kurt and his friends bribed their way back to Budapest to find their families. However, soon after his miraculous and joyous return home, the Hungarian Nazis seized political control of the nation. Kurt and his family knew that the Third Reich would soon move in and begin deporting Jews; the very existence of his family would be threatened. After painful deliberation, Kurt's parents decided to turn over their home and possessions to their neighbors for protection, and the three of them moved into a safe house. Safe houses were locations such as apartments, attics, or warehouses that could house up to 150 enemies of the Nazi state whose lives were at risk. For Jews and other "undesirables" under the swastika, safe houses were all that stood between them and probable death. In Budapest, Kurt, Ervin, and Zelma Bronner were taken into a safe house that was one of many set up by Swedish diplomat Raoul Wallenberg (a man who today is considered one of the great heroes of modern times for his courageous acts to save thousands of Jews from Hitler's death camps).

The Bronners' safe house was considered particularly secure because it was located in a dwelling over which flew the Swedish flag. But after only two weeks, an emerging power within Hungary—the Arrow Cross party—moved through Budapest like a steamroller, seeking out and destroying those who harbored "undesirables." It became extremely dangerous for the Hungarian people to harbor Jews at all. If discovered, they could be deported alongside those they had sought to rescue. Members of the Arrow Cross party marched through the streets in the late months of 1944, liquidating the safe houses and preparing their thousands of detainees for transport out of Hungary—and, unbeknownst to those arrested, to the death camps of Poland and Germany.

After their discovery and forced preparation to leave their beloved homeland, Kurt and his father—already separated from Zelma—were waiting to board the trains when Kurt saw a possible opening and begged his father to escape with him. Perhaps they could flee into the woods, or find shelter with a relative elsewhere? But Kurt's father, like many Jews who had been integrated into their countries in those days, could not begin to imagine the evil on the horizon. He told Kurt that they would just be taken to a labor camp, be forced to build roads or mine coal, and they would simply have to wait out the war. He was certain that the family would eventually be allowed to return to their home in

Budapest, where they would reclaim their property from their loyal neighbors. With this promise echoing in his ears, Kurt soon found himself in a cattle car with his father, beginning a journey into the farthest reaches of hell.

Inside each train car, wall-to-wall bodies struggled for space and room to move, flesh pressing hard up against flesh, as people strained for air in the suffocating confusion. The stench from the sweat, and from those who were losing control of their bodily functions, was nearly beyond endurance. After several days of travel they were allowed out into a snow-covered field, where they were able to relieve themselves, gulp fresh air, and roll out the corpses of those who had succumbed to the deadly conditions. The living were handed a single slice of bread and packed back into their inhumane prison for another five days of travel into darkness.

Kurt and his father were unknowingly on their way to the transit center known as Bergen-Belsen. It was here that tens of thousands of people would become victims of typhoid and starvation while waiting to be sent to the larger and even more deadly death camps in Poland. En route, Kurt and his father spoke desperately of Zelma. Where had they taken her? Would she be okay? Their fears overwhelmed them even as they struggled to hold on to one another, while all around them grown men wept and cries of despair echoed on the rails.

Upon arrival, Kurt and his father disembarked from their stifling cattle car, blinked into the harsh daylight, and took in the depraved setting that was Bergen-Belsen. How would they find Zelma in all of this? they thought in anguish? And from the first day, they began a nightmare of life circumscribed by the Nazi regimen. Each daybreak, the prisoners were expected to report for inspection outside their crude living quarters. One morning, Kurt awoke early. Though sleeping close to his father on the scant sheet of wood that was their bed, he was unusually cold that morning. Kurt heard some of his fellow prisoners chanting their

morning prayers. He asked them to quiet down, for his father was
still asleep and there were still a few moments until inspection.
He knew that his father could use all the rest he could manage.
One of the men turned to him with sad eyes and said softly:
"Kurt, your father is dead. He died during the night." Kurt turned
slowly, fearful to witness the sight of his father's body. Slowly it
dawned on him: this was the *cold* he had felt! Kurt sobbed into
the heartbreak of his father's lifeless body, rocking the two of
them as if he would never let go.

A short time later, Kurt stumbled from the inspection line to
which the others had dragged him. Lost in his mourning, Kurt
found himself by the barbed wire separating the women's quarters from the men, where he often went searching for his mother.
Incredibly, now, he looked up into the eyes of his mother. He felt
he would burst with the ache within him and the joy of seeing his
mother once again. They had not set eyes on one another since
the horror of leaving Budapest. His mother looked beaten down
with worry and hunger, but her features came alive instantly
when she saw her only son. But now she was searching frantically
behind him. "Kurt, where is Papa?" his mother asked anxiously.
Kurt could not bear to destroy his mother's hope that morning,
so he lied. "Papa is sleeping, Mama," he heard himself say, before
being separated yet again by guards. Kurt would never see his
mother again.

In April 1945, Bergen-Belsen was liberated by American soldiers. One of Kurt's first memories of liberation was being sprayed
with DDT by medical personnel to delouse the survivors. He was
taken to a former German Air Force officers' camp being used as a
temporary hospital by the Americans. He and ten others were
shown to a bedroom by one of the American officers, and Kurt
and the others piled in dutifully. The soldier looked bemused,
shaking his head. In English, which they had a hard time following, he tried to make clear that this was a bedroom for *one* man.
They would each get their own. After having spent so much time

crammed into claustrophobic spaces with so many others, the idea of having a room for oneself seemed beyond comprehension. Kurt's sense of awe, however, knew no bounds when he discovered that connected to this room was a private bathroom. "Do you know what dignity is?" Kurt suddenly thought. "Dignity is being allowed to go to the bathroom in privacy."

In the early stages of his recovery, Kurt chose to go back to Budapest in search of his mother. There was no trace of her. He soon discovered what he feared most: she had perished in the death camps. He returned to his old neighborhood, hoping to recover a few of his parents' possessions. But rather than offering the warmth of a homecoming, Kurt's old neighbors feigned ignorance. They insisted he was mistaken, that his mother and father had never left property with them. Kurt stared into their faces in disbelief. This young man, whose body and spirit had already experienced the deepest of wounds, now found his heart and soul lashed by this callous and outrageous betrayal.

An orphan of family and home, Kurt went to a displaced persons' camp where he earned his keep translating Hungarian and German documents. He was eventually transferred to Sweden with other survivors. There, on a blind date, he met a remarkable woman, Rosalie, who soon thereafter became his wife. She had been saved from the camps and brought to Sweden by a minister of the government. Kurt and Rosalie joined together, determined to weave a new life out of the horrors they both had known.

But the future would have to wait. While in Bergen-Belsen, Kurt had suffered a bout of pleurisy, which had affected his spine, and now he had to be hospitalized. He was forced to remain flat on his back in a Stockholm hospital for two full years. The doctors and nurses gave him the best care, and he was nurtured by their goodwill and expertise. Rosalie gave him hope and love, and his body and heart were, in time, nourished back to health.

In 1948, Kurt and Rosalie immigrated to Canada, and then eventually to Cleveland, Ohio. Here the two survivors brought two children into the world, helping one another to embrace life, and to thrive as individuals and as a family.

During their first year in Cleveland, before they'd come to know their neighbors very well, Kurt was approached by one of them with a simple request. There was a young family moving in down the street. They were new to the country, like the Bronners. It appeared that they spoke German and little English. Could Kurt and Rosalie take the young immigrants under their wing? Kurt agreed to do so with pleasure.

The Bronners invited the young couple, Hans and Ingrid, and their two little boys over to dinner, and together the group had a delightful time. The next night the young family reciprocated and the Bronners joined them for dinner at their home. Kurt and Rosalie were thrilled to have neighbors they could converse with in the language of the old country. After dinner, Hans brought out family photos and began sharing with Kurt pictures of his family home, his siblings, and his parents. As Kurt turned the pages of the family album, Hans regaled him with a richly enjoyable story about each photograph. Suddenly, Kurt turned to a new page and froze. Staring back at him was a photograph of a middle-aged man dressed in an SS uniform. Kurt began to shake involuntarily and, stammering an excuse about having forgotten to take care of a matter at home, he and Rosalie left abruptly.

The next day there was a knock on his door. It was the young husband. With great understanding and a blush of shame, he told Kurt he knew what must be troubling him. In the language of his birth, Hans explained softly. "You saw that photo of my father in uniform, and it deeply upset you. You must be Jewish. Am I right?" Kurt nodded. The young immigrant continued. "You were victims in the horror of the war? Yes, I am sure of it." Kurt swallowed hard. Hans went on, "Please, Mr. Bronner. You have to know. I am *not* my father. And I want to learn about Jews." And then, to Kurt's astonishment, he added, "Would you teach me?"

Kurt's mind flashed to the duplicitous neighbors who had

stolen his family's property. He remembered the suffering he had witnessed on the cattle car to Bergen-Belsen. He could see the lifeless form of his father on the morning he had died. He could make out in his heart's eye the face of his mother the last time he had seen her, through the barbed wire; the morning he had lied about his father to spare her pain. Visions of the living skeletons that gathered with him the morning their camp was liberated filled his head. The burning spray of DDT and the years on his back in the hospital flared in his mind's eye. Kurt looked into the young man's earnest face. This son of Germany was asking the survivor of his own father's cruelty for friendship. Kurt's wounds seemed to rise within him. Could he really befriend the son of an SS officer? He stood for a moment as if suspended, staring at Hans's outstretched hand. And then, moved by the pain of his burning memories and the simple request for redemption in front of him, Kurt took the young man's hand and welcomed him into his life.

The two families became good friends. Kurt, Rosalie, and their children shared dinners and holidays with Hans, Ingrid, and their boys. Hans was true to his word, making good on his desire to have his family learn more about the Jewish people. He could never make up for his father's deeds or the deeds of his fellow countrymen. But he could and would teach his own children that the Jewish people were their friends, and were possessed of a rich and treasured heritage. Kurt and Rosalie became like a mother and father to Hans and Ingrid, and like grandparents to their children. When it came time to select a preschool for the children, the young couple, to the Bronners' amazement, chose to send their children to a Jewish school. Kurt was overwhelmed. This young family was honoring his wounds. The children of his oppressors were deter-

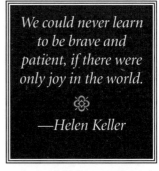

We could never learn to be brave and patient, if there were only joy in the world.

—Helen Keller

mined to give their own children the gift of humanity in learning to accept and respect the Bronners' way of life.

The following summer Hans and Ingrid took their children back to Germany to visit their families. The young man told Kurt later what had happened the day his father asked his grandchildren to sing a song they had learned in school. The children had burst simultaneously into a Hebrew folksong, *David Melech Yisrael.* Kurt imagined the face of the old SS officer, listening to his grandchildren singing in a language he had once tried to silence. And now his progeny had taken up a song that would not die. Kurt knew in his heart that he had brought honor and healing to his own—and his people's—wounds.

I first met Kurt a few years ago when he came to speak to a group of schoolchildren in California, where he and his family had moved long ago. Now in his seventies, with a full head of striking white hair, Kurt had begun speaking to children following the release of Steven Spielberg's movie of the Thomas Keneally book *Schindler's List.* For decades Kurt had chosen not to speak of these things, certainly never publicly. Now it was as if a silence in him had found its voice. He wanted to bear public witness to the atrocities, and to honor the memories of those who had perished. I watched with fascination from the back of the school synagogue as the children of the Heschel Day School drank in the quiet passion with which he spoke of his pain and loss.

As his words parted the air with living history, my eyes turned to a Torah scroll sitting in the latticed ark behind him. This was not just any scroll of the Five Books of Moses found in synagogues throughout the world. This one had been one of those targeted by Hitler's soldiers. It had been rescued from a burning synagogue in Czechoslovakia and was on loan from London's Westminster Synagogue. For some reason, I was compelled to take this burned and restored remnant of the Jewish people and place it in Kurt's arms. It seemed to bring something full circle.

Kurt's eyes filled with tears; his arms embraced the scroll as if it were a member of his family.

The children, teachers, and I looked on in hushed amazement at this *sacred* moment, one survivor holding another. Kurt later told me that it was one of the most moving moments of his life. He had felt the wounds within him—the loss of family, the injuries to his body and heart—soothed as he honored his memories and painful experiences. By holding that symbol of his people, Kurt was also holding the dearest parts of himself. And all of us bore witness to the light that filled that room.

Kurt has continued to bear witness through his accomplishments as a photographer. I marvel at the beauty he sees when he trains his camera on a world that has shown him such tragedy. In my study, I have one of his photographs; it is of a glorious flower opening to the sun, representing the simple act of celebrating life. It says a lot about a man, doesn't it? He can take the worst mankind is capable of and give back friendship, love, and the beauty of an unfolding flower.

Kurt has heard the voices of the family he lost, and those of the family he gained. He has heard the voices of the medical personnel who treated him and of those whose friendship he gained in his new country after the war. And he has heard the voice that poured out of his wounds, telling him that the ultimate honor he could give his suffering was in giving healing to others. And most profoundly, Kurt has made the most of the voices whispering to him to "*Grow, grow.*" He listened through the darkness, and he grew toward the light of family, love, and life. He is a light to all who know him.

———

Kurt's story, his art, and his actions tell me that we have a choice. What is it we wish to record as we look through the lens of our lives? Is what we choose to imprint and develop with the cameras of our hearts something that will do damage to the world? Is it something that will add to the *profane* in the universe? Are our choices going to bring it dignity and beauty, capturing something *sacred*? Will they bring hurt to others, or is it something that will help and heal? When we are motivated to see through the lens of our heart's camera and recognize a way to lift another's distress, then our souls are blessed.

It's our choice. We are the artists of our own lives and the life of the world as well. How and what we choose to see and embrace with our soul's eye determine how— or if—we honor our wounds and let them speak to us as *sacred* voices. Kurt found in his wounds a voice urging him to see and seize the *sacred* opportunity to comfort another person. He stepped into a new and powerful light that blessed him with passion and purpose. Sacred Wounds call the Kurts and Debrahs of the world to our assistance when we most need their healing. Through their example, they teach us how to grow toward a life of compassion and purposeful living and give back to the world. By taking *Step Six* and "honoring our wounds," we are assured that we and our pain *deserve no less*.

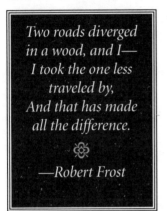

*Two roads diverged in a wood, and I—
I took the one less traveled by,
And that has made all the difference.*

—Robert Frost

HONORING WITH OUR DEEDS

I had the great privilege to be invited to Vienna in 2001 to interview one of the world's heroes of justice: Simon Wiesenthal. He is a man, like Kurt, who had suffered immense losses in the madness of the Holocaust. In 1945, Wiesenthal had weighed less than ninety pounds. He was barely alive when members of the U.S. forces liberated him from the Mauthausen concentration camp in Austria. Between his family and his wife Cyla's family, the Wiesenthals lost eighty-nine relatives.

Having miraculously survived Hitler's death squads, Wiesenthal explained to me, he became determined to pick up the pieces and rebuild his life. Before the war, he had been trained as an architect; it was his job to beautify communities. It was a vocation to which he desperately wished to return. But he had been approached by an American asking him to join a group that was gathering evidence against the Nazis. Wiesenthal told me: "We were naive. I thought, three years tops we find all the Nazis, round them up, and I go back to be an architect." Three years came and went, and Wiesenthal and others hadn't even begun to scratch the surface. The American who had talked him into this mission of justice fell in love and returned home to the States. Wiesenthal smiled as he related this turn of events: "Well, you know, love—it happens," he said with a wink.

Wiesenthal had a choice to make: he could follow his heart and go back to the architect's life he wanted so badly to live. After all, who could blame him? He had given three years of his life to this impossible quest. But Wiesenthal knew the other choice would haunt him. He could see in his conscience the suffering of his family, his wife, himself. And he could feel the gaze of those who had perished peering over his shoulder. The only way to honor the wounds of his life and those who had suffered was to continue on this mission of bringing about justice for criminal acts against humanity. And for the last fifty-six years, that is exactly what he has done. He has painstakingly documented the cruelty and crimes of the Nazis, amassing evidence to bring them to trial and speaking out for those who no longer have a voice.

For Wiesenthal, this was never about revenge. It has always been about justice. By passionately honoring his own wounds, he responded to the wounds of others. And by doing so, Wiesenthal transformed his life and helped illuminate the world, insisting by example that injustice demands action, not silence. William Butler Yeats once warned: "The ceremony of innocence is drowned. The best lack all conviction, while the worst are full of passionate intensity." Wiesenthal proved that it could be another way, that the best, too, could use their passion for justice and restore a measure of honor to the world.

On August 9, 2000, President Clinton honored Simon Wiesenthal with the Presidential Medal of Freedom, the highest civilian award in the United States. In a statement issued from Vienna where he lives and continues to work, Wiesenthal said:

"For half a century, I have worked on more than 1,100 cases involving Nazi war criminals, bringing to justice the commandants of Treblinka and Sobibor death camps, the inventor of the mobile gas vans, and the individual who arrested Anne Frank. My cause was justice, not vengeance. My work is for a better tomorrow and a more secure future for our children and grandchildren.

"As a believer that all of us are accountable before our Creator, I have always believed that when my life is over, I shall meet up with those who perished, and they will ask me, 'What have you done?' At that moment, I will have the honor of telling them, I have never forgotten you."

When I asked Wiesenthal what he wished to convey to a world in search of honor, he responded: "I am no hero. I do what I know I must. I wish for there to not be only one Simon Wiesenthal. I should not be special. That many should stand for justice."

Wiesenthal ennobles us all by showing the power and energy of human commitment when we honor the wounds that have disfigured our bodies, our hearts, and our souls. I will never forget the moment when Simon Wiesenthal took my nine-month-old daughter, Shira, into his arms. This man who had suffered the lacerations of the Third Reich, who had experienced starvation, the murder of family members, forced labor, beatings, attempts on his life. He gently cupped her face in his hand, kissing her tiny fingers repeatedly. His face was filled with complete and utter joy.

When we recognize the immense challenges that people like Kurt Bronner and Simon Wiesenthal have faced, we know more

clearly the depth of a human being's ability to respond to wounds
by honoring his or her actions. We might hear again the question
put to Debrah: "What do you want to do with your life?" Perhaps
some of us will answer by reaching out to secure the future of
others. We might let go of the guilt of our past actions that continue to wound us and, like Brad, recognize that each of us
deserves joy; we then might help spread joy for those who need it.
We might drain away the *profane* shadows of illness, as Lena did,
and transform pain into power and power into light so others can
know just how precious life really is. We might celebrate the
sacred within our wounds by honoring those who brought us
healing. How best can we honor those who have shown compassion to us? By helping to heal those in need right now.

The light that pours forth from our response can illuminate
not only our own hearts but those of the people we will touch, as
the miller taught the farmer. For, in honoring our wounds, we
whisper in word and deed our message of affirmation to the
world: "*Grow, grow.*"

———

THE TASK

In your journal, you are going to make a list.

Take time to recall the person(s) who stepped forward or
came into your life as a result of your having been wounded. Perhaps it was someone you already knew—a family member, a close
friend, a member of the clergy. Or it might have been someone
from the medical profession who was treating you—a therapist, a
member of a support group, a nurse or doctor. Maybe it was
someone you met in a yoga or gym class. If you can't think of
anyone right away, think again. Did you get

❀ a phone call from an old acquaintance who heard about
   your loss?

❀ an e-mail from a classmate that turned into a regular correspondence?

❀ a hug from a nurse, flowers or a card from a spouse, child, or friend?

❀ simply a look of understanding from someone who just knew the pain you were feeling?

Write about one of these encounters. What was said or done *to* you and *for* you because of your wound? How did it make you feel at the time? How does it sit in your soul now?

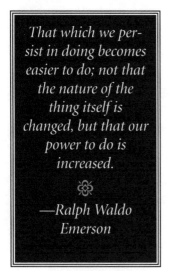

That which we persist in doing becomes easier to do; not that the nature of the thing itself is changed, but that our power to do is increased.

—Ralph Waldo Emerson

Is there any gift you could give right now to someone in need? What is that person's pain? How can you relate to him or her more deeply because you've experienced your own wounds? What would it mean to that person to have you show compassion? What would it mean to the way you see yourself? Can you see the *sacred* in this exchange? Write about it.

Remember the words of the miller: *life is like the water wheel that helps me grind my grain. It all moves in a circle.*

THE RITUAL

Kurt found a great emotional release in the light he saw the moment he wrapped his arms around the Holocaust Torah. There was a healing and an honoring of the losses he had suffered, for he was blessing the memory of those who had suffered with him.

❀ Select an object that has deep emotional meaning for you, one that you associate with your wound: a diary, a photograph, a family heirloom, an article of clothing, a letter.

❁ As you hold your object, express appreciation for your own endurance as you experienced your wounds. Recall another person you were motivated to help as a result of your pain. If you have not had this experience, resolve now to reach out to someone or a group that could use your compassion. Honor this awareness and these actions you have and will yet take. Taking up the emotional object, hold it as if it represented all you feel you have lost. Cradle it, treasure it, and feel compassion for what you have been through. Let it inspire you to spread that compassion to others in the world.

THE GIFT

We affirm that our *miracles of self-knowledge* can be used to honor the injuries of others and, as with Kurt's photographs of nature, to bring beauty into the world:

❁ There are voices of angels in my life that have urged me to grow when I didn't feel it was possible. I honor their caring actions.

❁ When I respond to another's pain, I not only honor these human angels, I become one myself.

❁ My endurance is a tribute to my own inner strength and bestows honor upon the soul that lives within me.

❁ I can choose how I will record the world through the lens of my heart's camera. When I see and celebrate what can help and heal the world, rather than what can hurt it, I bring affirmation to my life and the lives of others.

❁ Honoring my wounds means allowing them to help me make a difference in the world. Each of us can bring about healing. Each of us is *that* powerful.

Giving tribute to those who have made a difference in our lives motivates us to live a life worthy of our wounds. Like Kurt

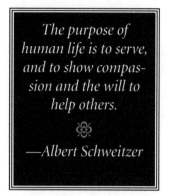

The purpose of human life is to serve, and to show compassion and the will to help others.

—*Albert Schweitzer*

Bronner, we can face what we have endured and reach beyond the pain and darkness to inspire growth in others. Like Simon Wiesenthal, we can recognize that our wounds need justice to be honored. In *Step Six*, we have seen that our Sacred Wounds can galvanize us into action, honoring not only our own pain but that of others. And we can use that energy to light the path to a more just and honorable world.

Step Seven will help us learn to take our purposeful living and turn our ongoing quest for success into a journey of hope. It is that very optimism that will take us one step closer to empowerment and the triumph it can bring.

Kurt would join me in an affirmation that is also a destination: there's no place like *hope*.

Step Seven

EMBRACING THE HOPE: Integrating a Knowing Optimism

> *Optimism is essential to achievement and it is also*
> *the foundation of courage and true progress.*
> —Nicholas Murray Butler

THE MEDITATION
As I sit in the palm of my understanding,
Aware of the knowledge born of my pain,
May I possess the insight to use my gifts
To enrich my world and that of others.

By turning healing into hope,
Wisdom into action,
Openness into wonder.
Weaving the lessons I've been given
Into the contours of my spirit,
May I move ever forward
To the destiny that is mine.

———

The Taoists have a saying: My barn having burned to the ground, I can now see the moon.

In taking *Step Six* and "honoring our wounds," we have discovered *purposeful living* and have moved forward on our journey toward success. By using the awareness that our lives can be deeper, richer, and more meaningful when we journey with a sense of empathy and perform acts of compassion, we can create a higher consciousness, opening wide the door of optimism within ourselves. This leads us to *Step Seven*, in which we will weave the lessons of our wounded spirit into our quest to claim the success we desire. Integrating knowledge acquired from our wounds into our daily lives, into our mind, heart, and hands, not only encourages hope but becomes itself *an act of hope.*

Using the wisdom, the precious path, and this higher purpose to inform our daily choices allows us to weave the understanding and hope born of our pain into the tapestry of our evolving self. This knowledge and optimism are all the more cherished because they came at a cost. Just as a fire cuts a swath through the forest, leaving loss and destruction in its wake, it also enriches the soil so that the wounded trees can renew their strength, making real the hope of rejuvenation. Similarly, integrating understanding and hope into our everyday lives renews and rejuvenates us. It reveals the best part of who we are, which can only be produced by an open heart and a burnished spirit. Such an optimistic heart and spirit emerge once we discover that there is a purpose in our pain that allows *healing to turn to hope.* The creation of this hope is one of the key outcomes of purposeful living. Yet it is a *knowing optimism*—infused with wisdom, passion, and direction. Integrating this brand of hope into our journey creates for us a road map to our destination.

HOPE IS HEALTHY

*D*r. Martin E. P. Seligman, author of *Learned Optimism*, argues that acquiring the mind-set of hope is essential to our health. Seligman states that pessimists can be shown statistically to encounter more negative experiences, including illness, than optimists: "Because [pessimists] are more passive, they are less likely to take steps to avoid bad events and less likely to do anything to stop them once they start." This is not to say that optimists will not encounter pain, but it does suggest that they don't compound their wounds with unnecessary suffering that they might have avoided had they lived a more hopeful and proactive life.

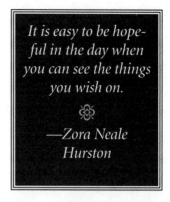

It is easy to be hopeful in the day when you can see the things you wish on.

—Zora Neale Hurston

How do you like that—*hope is good for our health!* Embracing hope is essential to the full realization of the power of our Sacred Wounds. The beauty here is that weaving optimism created by our pain into our everyday living can help direct us away from future wounds and toward a life blessed with a stronger vision, purposeful living, and beliefs that support our dreams.

When, for example, we consciously apply our past experience in an abusive relationship to the choice of a new partner, we are resisting a sorrowful recycling of old pain, and integrating the wisdom of our wounding into everyday life choices. This, in turn, creates hope for the success we seek. It is hope fostered by knowledge, an understanding produced from our painful experiences. When we consciously apply our childhood experience with a parent's abandonment to our own parenting, we are teaching ourselves that the past doesn't equal the future. We weave into our self-perception the optimistic understanding that we are *not* our father or mother. Drawing on these lessons and putting them into action affirms who we are today and who we choose to become. And it is all the more *sacred* for having been born of our wounds.

As we move through *Step Seven,* we integrate this knowing optimism produced by our wounds into the choices we make and

> Each person has
> inside a basic decency
> and goodness.
> If he listens to it
> and acts on it, he is
> giving a great deal
> of what it is the
> world needs most.
> It is not complicated
> but it takes courage.
> It takes courage
> for a person to listen
> to his own goodness
> and act on it.
>
> ❀
>
> —Pablo Casals

the values we have adopted. For instance, imagine being among friends when someone makes a racial or gender slur that gets your heart beating like a band—or offers up some malicious gossip about a person's looks, intellectual capacity, or gender that has the same effect. In the past, you may have swallowed your discomfort, indeed may never have spoken up for what you believed. But now the blessing of your wound illuminates your choice. It's what causes you to speak out. That's the person you were meant to be—someone who contributes kindness and dignity and truth and makes a positive difference in the lives around you. You will not allow hurtful comments to go unchallenged, or enable someone to denigrate the human spirit. You speak the truth, and stand up for what you believe. *And what we believe is virtually worthless if it remains dormant within us.*

Just as you allowed the experience and pain of your wound to touch you profoundly, so you now possess the ability to use them to illuminate even the smallest corners of the world. That is hope personified. It crowns the purposeful living of *Step Six* with the actualization of the hero within us. Knowing optimism not only helps bring out all of our potential, it challenges the world to do the same. Because there is a transformation within us when we incorporate the understanding and hope that comes to light out of past suffering. It is the emergence of confidence in who we are and wish to be. This involves more than acquiring a sense of purpose, it is inhabiting our lives with the powerful hope that says "I know who I am, I know what I stand for, I know what I value, and I will act from that core of conviction." This burnished sense of self is the road map for the journey to success, for when it is actualized, its knowing optimism will keep our quest on track.

Step Seven takes us beyond honoring our wounds through acts of compassion to transforming our lives and those of others by fashioning the world of optimism in which we choose to live. When we encounter social circumstances like the one just cited, we will recognize one of two things—either we're truly among friends and our truth will count for something, or we'll discover we weren't among friends after all. Those who deny our right to speak our heart, or who laugh at our truth, have little place in our world of life-affirming success. The cost of their negativity is one we ought to refuse to pay. And we can live with that. In fact, we can live *better* with that. Having made the choice of what is true and good within us, and learned what truly resonates within our soul, we can stop living behind a mask. We can take our conviction, our goodness, and our hope, and boldly build pontoons or bridges that will ensure the completion of our journey.

As we've seen earlier, it takes self-awareness to integrate the understanding and hope of our wounds consciously and effectively into our lives. It takes knowledge of where we've been and recognition of the signals that lead us to make negative choices. When we recognize that we *can* make different choices, healthier and positive ones, then we find that our pain can produce purpose in our lives and build hope for our future.

LET YOUR POWER PROMPT YOU

One of the ways we can add such knowing optimism into the everyday dynamic of our lives is to approach each of our significant decisions with *power prompts*. These questions help prompt us to examine whether we are following the hard-earned knowledge of what best serves our own heart and dreams, which is the source of hope. They can help identify actions that may be contrary to what can foster our success. This enhances our journey, for that which gets in the way of our success, as we know, produces pain rather than hope. We've come this far, why would we step backward?

In essence, *power prompts* can serve as a simple gauge of whether or not we are deliberately acting as the *authors of our own destiny*. Having accepted the wisdom of our wounds, claimed the path it revealed, and started a journey of purposeful living, are we making effective use of their lessons?

Here, then, are five examples of *power prompts* we can use while making decisions:

- ❀ Does this choice *limit* or *enhance* who I am and who I want to be?
- ❀ Does this choice provide clarity, helping me to define success for myself, or does it make that success harder to see?
- ❀ Does this choice help me live by my values, or is it an obstacle to them?
- ❀ Am I listening to any warning signals that might be telling me there is danger ahead, or is this choice in harmony with what I know is best for me?
- ❀ Does this choice come about out of pessimism and fear, or is it born of my *hopes*?

While it may not always be possible to press the pause button in life and activate these *power prompts,* they can certainly serve as the basis for important, life-altering decisions. Using *power prompts* when facing significant forks in the road can not only assist us in integrating our wounds' knowing optimism into our decisions and values, but doing so will gradually incorporate them into every-

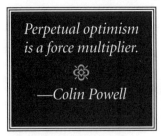

Perpetual optimism is a force multiplier.

❀

—Colin Powell

day decision-making processes, and ultimately become second nature.

BEING MINDFUL IS KEY

Power prompts are excellent tools to help us examine our decision-making rationally. Another channel for effectively integrating the knowledge and hope of our wounds is to be mindful of our unique *emotional signals*. Following these signals is like navigating by the stars. Recognizing random formations isn't enough. We must know what the formations *mean* in relation to the direction we want to follow. Recall Kurt's story in *Step Six:* how he felt in facing the son of a Nazi was based on the devastating wounds he and others had suffered. Intuitively, he didn't want to continue the *cycle* of this wound, and so chose hope over hate. Kurt's decision to take this path of friendship turned his pain into possibility, and his healing into hope.

One of the challenges of integrating the lessons our wounds have gifted us, then, is that it requires a certain *mindfulness* in dealing with our emotions. We may have been on a nonstop ride down the road of existence until our wounds threw on the brakes, leaving us immobile in a fog of fear and frazzled emotions, shaking us from the world we had always known. Molly Ivins, a breast cancer survivor and a first-rate writer/political columnist, put it this way in *Time* magazine: "I tend to treat my emotions like unpleasant relatives—a long-distance call once or twice a year is more than enough. If I got in touch with them, they might come to stay."

Being mindful of our emotions allows them to embrace the hope that is key to our success. Integrating this knowing optimism includes heightening our consciousness of how our emotions affect us. Past experiences have taught us which emotional messages harm us, and which can elevate our hopefulness and encourage our success. The lessons we derive from our pain help us to

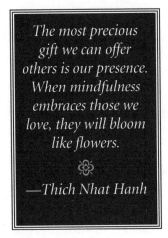

The most precious gift we can offer others is our presence. When mindfulness embraces those we love, they will bloom like flowers.

—Thich Nhat Hanh

employ an *emotional sunscreen.* Choosing to integrate and implement what we have learned provides us with a buffer capable of keeping out the harmful rays of *profane* and destructive influences while opening us up to *sacred* and restorative influences.

In the past, as adults, we may have been subjected to emotional abuse from a family member or lover. From our passive reaction to such behavior, they learned that we would cower and give them their way. In such cases, our hardened emotional shell provided no protection from the abuse directed at us. But integrating the knowledge and hope of our wounds can actually shield us from these hits to our self-esteem and human worth. By instilling within ourselves the *core belief* that we deserve to be treated with respect and dignity and that we actually *can* do something about it, we can protect our hearts and empower our minds.

Being shielded by *emotional sunscreen* is possible once we realize the full dimensions of optimism and hope that our wisdom has unleashed within us. If we are to

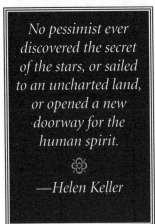

No pessimist ever discovered the secret of the stars, or sailed to an uncharted land, or opened a new doorway for the human spirit.

—Helen Keller

gain maximum benefit from these forces of hope, it is essential that we keep building on the lessons we've learned. Staying *connected to hope* is a conscious choice—one that will feed and nourish that place within us that harbors our Sacred Wounds and our sacred dreams.

Twenty-five hundred years ago, the Greek playwright Aeschylus wrote: "Even in our sleep, pain that cannot forget falls drop by drop upon the heart and in our own despair, against our will, comes wisdom to us by the awful grace of God." Sooner or later, pain has a way of breaking through the mighty barriers we may have constructed in front of our hearts. And wisdom may be acquired even when we have not welcomed it. But this wisdom can never be integrated into our lives—it can never serve our soul and our spirit—*against our will*. It is with mindfulness and hope that we consciously apply the lessons of our wounds to the lives we are living and to the success we are creating.

———

I want to tell you the story of a woman who struggled with pessimism born of a major life's wound that all of us, in one way or another, will experience. Her hard-fought renewal of life and hope came only when she learned from the pain of her loss that she had the power to fulfill her own destiny.

Clare's Story

*H*olding on to the photograph of her late husband, Clare was racked with loneliness. It had been seven months since his death, and yet she asked the same questions over and over: how could Charles have left her so early? He was the love of her life. No. He *was* her life. He filled her with purpose. Who would do that for her now?

They had been married right out of college. Charles was stationed in Norfolk, Virginia, where he served as a lieutenant in the Navy. There Clare developed strong bonds with other Navy wives. After he left the service, they navigated themselves into the busy world of children and career. Charles had majored in business, and upon returning to his hometown in New England had taken a position in the business affairs office of the local university. Clare and their two children would soon become an integral part of university life. They never missed the opportunity to enjoy the annual snow sculpture competition, take part in the winter carnival, or attend Oktoberfest with its pumpkin designs, hot apple cider, and fresh-made doughnuts. They also regularly attended musical performances, staff picnics, and, of course, commencement festivities. Clare loved watching Charles lead his staff and students in the traditional graduation sing-along at midnight on the campus green.

Charles was so good at what he did that he had been selected repeatedly for advancement, rising eventually to a vice-presidency in the university. In the dead of winter, when he would have to trudge off to some official event, he used to joke that he was actually the "*ice*-president." Clare and Charles had found the joy of living a full life in each other's company.

As their children grew up, attended the university, and moved out, Charles and Clare began a life of long walks, good food by a hearty fire, and the joy of travel. Most of their longtime friends had moved on to other colleges or migrated to retirement in warmer climates. Clare talked occasionally to Charles about taking a sabbatical to France, Italy, or some exotic place while they were still able to do so, and he would promise, as he always did, that they'd do it "next year." As the years passed, Clare took up a few outside activities, but she was generally content to stay at home, cultivate her flowers, do some knitting, and wait for Charles to come home, where he would share the day's news and adventures as she provided ongoing whimsical commentary.

On a crisp, clear winter day in March, Clare was preparing Charles's lunch when the phone rang. Charles had collapsed outside the administration building on his way home, she was told. Though he had been rushed immediately to the hospital, it was too late. Without ever regaining consciousness, he had died of a coronary. Clare collapsed to the floor in shock; she was still there when Charles's longtime assistant, who had rushed over in grief after hearing the news, revived her, and brought her to the hospital.

Their daughter, Julia, had stayed with Clare for the first week after her father's burial, but had to return to her children back in Seattle. Their son, Michael, took care of the financial arrangements, and made provisions for the university benefits to come to his mother before he left to rejoin his young family in Atlanta. As the weeks wore on, the calls of well-wishing and support subsided, and the letters and cards from former colleagues and students receded to a trickle before stopping altogether. Before she knew it, she was left with her memories and her grief.

Why did this happen? she wondered. Like herself, Charles had been just fifty-nine years old. He had been sick only rarely, and there had been no indication that he was in any kind of health danger. They had so much living left to do! Her dreams of growing old with him would never be fulfilled. Instead, she was alone.

The thought and weight of her loss overwhelmed her. Now, alone in the empty house, Clare cried often, staring at Charles's place across the table or the void in her bed. It seemed impossible that the life and love she had known could be torn from her with such a cruel finality. She often cradled her husband's photograph in her hands, moving through her pain at a slow pace and with no destination. The word "widow" crossed her mind and she flinched, rejecting even the sound of the label with a hard shake of her head.

The weeks and months passed, and Clare experienced many smaller deaths with the turning of the seasons and the constant reminder that Charles would never again share them with her. At first she went out only to pick up a few groceries, replenish her plant supplies, or occasionally for the chai tea with cinnamon that Charles used to bring home to her on chilly autumn afternoons. With the passage of time, however, she began taking walks that seemed to soothe her, took in the occasional Saturday afternoon film, and slowly began to reemerge into life.

Clare was doing the things she had always taken for granted when Charles was around—paying the bills, getting the house painted when the exterior was chipping, contacting repairmen when needed. She went to visit her children and grandchildren during the next summer and felt the warmth of being with family. She was healing, she told them. She was going about the business of life again. Still, Clare felt an emptiness within her. It was true that she was functioning again, but she was lost, and the experience of joy—sustained and regenerating—seemed no more than a distant memory.

It was after getting her tea on a cold October day seven months after Charles died that Clare encountered a woman she remembered from some of the university functions she and Charles had attended together. She was perhaps ten or fifteen years older than Clare, and was dressed in a cloak that made her appear distinctly Elizabethan. The stranger invited her to sit down by the fire roaring in the tearoom. Clare began to make an excuse, but the woman persisted.

After a few niceties, the stranger explained that she, too, was a widow. Her husband had been chairman of the theater department for years (that explains the costume, thought Clare). She had taught communications for some time before she and her husband had decided to move to England for a sabbatical; they had simply grown so fond of the place, they decided to remain. After his death several years ago, she decided that it was time to come home. She had known Charles—not well, but enough to share a conversation whenever they bumped into each other crossing the campus. He was a good man, she told Clare warmly, and it must have been a terrible loss.

Clare looked away, not eager to prolong the conversation, but still pleased to hear the woman speak so highly of Charles. Noticing Clare's distant gaze, the lady abruptly asked a strange question: "You haven't returned, have you?"

Clare looked back at her in confusion. "I beg your pardon?" she asked.

"From the isle of mourning."

"The isle of . . . what?" Clare wasn't sure she liked this stranger.

"I've been there. I know the island well," she told Clare almost dreamily. "I know the ebb and flow of its surrounding waters. The sleepless nights, the loneliness of a castaway. The emptiness and broken dreams. Yes, I was stuck on that island for a long time." The woman took a long sip of her tea, which she held in both hands, warming them.

This was a presumptuous imposition, Clare thought angrily. Who did this person think she was, talking to her about Charles in such an intimate manner? This pain belonged to her. And yet there was something about the stranger's warm smile, the knowing way in which she held her gaze. Clare found she couldn't look away or bring herself to get up and leave.

"I know, I know, it's not my business, you're thinking. Who's this old biddy anyway to tell me what I've lost, right?" The woman grinned, and almost chuckled. Clare smiled back, nodding at having been caught.

"I felt the same when my husband died," she went on, her smile growing broader. "It was a private grief, and I would allow no one else to share it. But after some time I realized that staying on that island of sadness and solitary living was a way of hiding out from the life I had left. And what's more . . . it was destroying all the good and happy memories my husband and I had built together. That wasn't fair to him. And it wasn't fair to who I was when I was with him. Does that make sense?"

Clare smiled sadly and looked down. It did. She had been a joyous person with Charles. She had loved their trips, the school functions, dinners in front of the fire. His spirit had filled her with laughter, and joy and hope, and she loved who she was when she was with him. Now all her memories of the things they had done together were marked with a profound sorrow, which discolored them and bled the life from them.

The woman watched Clare with a soft gaze and then went on to explain that one day she began to figure out how she might lead herself back to the joy she had shared with her husband. Although she could never replace their special bond, she said, she *could* celebrate it by living her own life as fully as she knew he would want her to, and by putting something of their love back into the world. "Do you know what I mean?" she asked Clare. "I just realized I was letting him down by not taking care of *myself*!" This last thought struck Clare particularly strongly, for now she *did* know exactly what she meant.

The woman told Clare that one day she had recognized how far her pain had taken her from real living. "I was just reliving the pain, stuck in old memories, recycling everything we'd ever done together in my mind, when suddenly this child knocked on my door to sell me some candy. She told me it was for a future trip her scout group was going to be taking. I realized right there that I had lost even the *idea* of a future, and that it was something my husband would never have accepted. How could *I* accept it?"

The lady went on to explain to Clare that she'd come to the realization that life was not permanent. What mattered, however, was how strong her connection to living really was, and that the connection didn't have to die with her husband. In fact, it would be an insult to his memory if it did. One of the strongest lessons of sadness, the woman explained, was that grief didn't fit with who she was or who she was meant to be.

"But how did you manage to do all this?" Clare asked. "I feel so lost even now. And Charles has been gone for over seven months!"

The woman sighed and nodded. "Hmm—yes, it wasn't easy. But I remember that one thing I did was write about all my feelings. I laid them out there so I could take a good hard look at them and not hide from them anymore. I'd ask myself questions right alongside these feelings. I wrote down all the things I had done with my husband that had made me happy. I asked myself to remember what I had accomplished on my own that made me feel good about who I was. It helped me to write lists like that, because I was already forgetting so much, you know?"

Clare nodded, feeling as if she might cry. She *did* know that feeling of forgetting and how afraid it made her.

The woman continued. "I'd also ask little questions of myself, like 'What gives me pleasure?' 'What is important to me?' 'What do I want to learn?' 'How can I live in a loving way?' " The woman paused, smiling. "When I heard answers to those questions, it didn't matter if I was in the shower or on the phone—I'd head directly to that journal and write them all down there."

Clare thought for a moment and then spoke. "I keep thinking I'm healed, but I don't feel any joy. Sometimes it's like I'm beyond—I don't know . . . hope. Did you . . . do you feel that way?"

"I'll tell you something," the woman replied. "I felt that way a lot. That's why I started making a list of all the good things I saw or experienced or could think of each day. This meant I had to notice what was going on around me, not hide out on the island I'd been living on. I called it my 'checklist of hope,' and it has become quite important to me. I'm still adding to it. In fact, you'll make my list today when I get home."

Clare was surprised, "Me? Why would I be on a list of hope? I'm just listening!"

The woman smiled, and leaned forward as if to share a great secret. "Yes. Just because of that," she said, her eyes lighting up. "Because you stopped to listen." Later, alone at home, the woman's words still echoed for Clare. As she moved around the hothouse and the plants in which she had always taken such joy, Clare thought about the woman's words—"life was not permanent." Yes, that is true, thought Clare, imagining Charles beaming at her as he always did when he found her toiling away in the garden with soil and seeds. It was as if she could hear his voice, but she knew it was her own. "No, life may not be permanent," she could hear herself saying, "but love *is*." She suddenly had the urge to write that down, even to call the woman. Then it dawned on Clare—she hadn't even asked the lady her name!

That night, standing naked before the mirror in her bedroom, Clare examined not only her body, but her soul. She asked the questions that had been haunting her for months. How could Charles have left her so early? He had filled her life with purpose. Who would do that for her now? And the answer emerged in a voice that came from within her pain—*she* would have to fill her life with purpose. *She was her own best destiny.*

Clare went out the next morning and bought a journal. Following the advice of the woman in the tearoom, each day she wrote out every feeling she was experiencing and then questioned them. "What does this tell me about how hopeful I'm acting?" "How can I change and be more open?" "What do I want to accomplish?" "How can my emotions help support me?" She began to discover that her sadness had a great deal to teach her, not only about what she *didn't* have but what she *did* have. For instance, she knew she didn't have Charles to arrange to have the water pipes repaired when they burst during a cold snap, but she *did* have a good neighbor who had taken her in, stuffing her with fresh-baked cookies and talking with her on into the night until the pipes could be repaired.

She would list all the qualities of her life that she had valued when Charles was alive. At first she noticed that Charles's qualities dominated her pages. Soon, however, she was identifying more and more of her own characteristics, such as patience and perseverance. Whenever the family hit a roadblock, she was the one who rallied their resources and found a way. Charles liked to say that she could always manage to turn a no into a yes.

The more Clare recorded, the more she began to learn that the deep pain she had been experiencing, and the distancing from life it had precipitated, had diminished the qualities of her life—and she was the poorer for it. At the same time, her loss and loneliness could remind her of who she had once been and how she could continue to feel most connected to Charles—and to life. The belief that her life was over had been incorrect—and now she realized that she could change that belief. In her newfound awareness, she was coming to see that her life wasn't over; her pain was pushing her to ever new horizons of personal growth. This pain now urged her forward, reminding her that she *could* fill her sense of emptiness by choosing to live life with joy and gusto.

Clare remembered what the woman had told her about a "checklist of hope." She began jotting down images and events that filled her with optimism about her life and future. Her phone conversations with her children and grandchildren reminded her that she was far from alone. The glorious autumn leaves not only offered beauty, but carried with them the message that, though they might fall away before the winter, they would return in the spring and begin the cycle anew.

One day, Clare returned from a foray out in the neighborhood and found a book on her doorstep. It was a copy of Shakespeare's *The Tempest*, and it bore an inscription taken from the play: "*We are such stuff as dreams are made on. . . .* " To those words a personal note was added: "*To hot tea, warm fires, and the future.*" The note was signed *Miranda*. Gratefully, Clare added this touching gesture to her checklist of hope.

Clare was so grateful for her fortunate meeting with Miranda that she contacted her, and soon the two began sharing weekly tea and gab sessions. Miranda taught Clare about England and Shakespeare, and Clare taught Miranda about the joy of raising hothouse plants and cultivating vegetables.

Walking across campus with Miranda one spring afternoon, Clare saw a sign asking for volunteers at the university child-care center. Here was an opportunity she would never have noticed or been interested in just six months earlier. Now, however, it *did* interest her.

It didn't take long for Clare to make a name for herself as "the plant lady" and to become a permanent fixture at the center. Sharing her passion for growing new life, Clare created a children's garden in the middle of the campus quad. The class tended it with her every other day, and the university honored the project with its beautification award. In giving to the children, Clare received in return the delight of the young life that surrounded her. She had known this kind of connection only through her own children and grandchildren. Now she was experiencing it every day. In a unique way, Charles was alive in her teaching and in her new role on campus.

On the anniversary of Charles's death, Clare went alone to the cemetery. From her journal, she read aloud all that she had learned about loneliness, healing, and hope. She shed tears of sadness and of thanksgiving. And she placed a living plant at the foot of his grave. She told him of her new sense of purpose with the day-care children. Miranda was even urging her to go back to school and complete an advanced degree in teaching. She promised him, even in moments when she felt his absence the most, that she would always renew the hope she had felt during the twenty-eight years he had loved her. Clare had found her *life-right*—wisdom based on the rocky but ultimately regenerating path of experience.

Later that day, Miranda found a plant on her doorstep. The attached note began with a quote Clare had found in a book of inspiration Charles had tried to get her to read. It read: *"If I am not for myself, who will be for me? But if I am only for myself, what am I? And if not now, when?"* These were the words of a man named Hillel who had lived thousands of years ago. And Clare completed the inscription with a personal note: *"Thanks for helping me answer these questions . . . and for showing me the way off the island."*

After her name, Clare scribbled in bold letters—*"I'm glad to be back."*

For Clare, the way back to the *mainland of life* was found by carefully listening to and incorporating the knowledge her pain had given her. By integrating the lessons of hope, generated by a friend's intervention and her own hard work, she didn't have to remain isolated on an island of misery and depression. By reaffirming her connection to pleasure, growth, joy, and perseverance, she uncovered the optimism that had been missing in her outlook since Charles's death. By embracing a positive worldview, she honored her husband and the bond they had spent years forging together. Most important, she regained her sense of purpose and came to recognize that the power to act on that purpose was *within* her. Much to her surprise and infinite pleasure, Clare learned that she loved herself enough to make use of that power and awareness and claim a new path of *knowing optimism.*

INTEGRATING WISDOM AND HOPE
INTO OUR DAILY LIVES

*A*s we have seen over and over again, finding hope and light in the wake of loss and darkness requires a conscious choice to be mindful of the positive emotional signals within us. It is a skill that many artists carefully cultivate when creating art that simultaneously poses questions about the world we live in while depicting the beauty and truth of the human condition, the natural world, or the puzzling and terrible beauty of both. I've been privileged to know one such artist who taught me immeasurable lessons about the search for hope by the way he integrated the lessons of his own considerable wounds. His quest to portray the

While there's life,
there's hope.

—Cicero

depth and beauty of our flawed humanity in light of unfath-
omable suffering is also a journey to discover the wisdom of our
collective wounds and their power to turn healing into hope.

I was in my late twenties when I was chosen to star as Zalman
in the second American production of Elie Wiesel's play on identity and loss, *Zalman, or the Madness of God.* Wiesel, the winner
of the 1995 Nobel peace prize and author of dozens of books on
suffering and hope, has long represented the epitome of the
wounded heart that refuses to turn its pain inward; instead, he
bears witness for others through his many thoughtful and challenging books, his mesmerizing teaching, and, in this case, his
drama. His survival as a teenager in Auschwitz has been the backdrop to much of his life's work as a writer, university professor,
and social activist. On the night of my debut, I was privileged to
count Wiesel among the members of my audience.

The play is set in a small town in Russia in the late sixties,
when dissidents were jailed (or worse) for simply trying to maintain their identities. The drama deals with how the spirit of Jewish life was crushed under Soviet rule; the action centers on
Zalman, an eccentric caretaker of a dying synagogue. Early in the
play, Zalman tries to convince an elderly rabbi into publicly bearing witness to their collective suffering in front of several visiting
Americans. The threats of the Communist secret police notwith-
standing, Zalman manages to convince the rabbi to speak out.
Afterward, the characters wonder what the rabbi's defiance will
mean. Will it change anything?

Wiesel's play also features a character who is the son of a
Communist and the grandson of the rabbi. The question arises
whether the boy will choose to identify with his father, a man
who has become a Communist party official and turned his back
on his roots in order to avoid being shunned, or elect to have a
bar mitzvah, an act that would connect him explicitly with his
grandfather and his people's embattled identity. At the end of the
play the boy rushes from a room, and we hear his father calling

his name—"Misha, Misha!" He is running in one direction, he has made a choice, but the audience doesn't know if he is racing toward his father or his grandfather. Wiesel deliberately leaves the question of Misha's future open. Did Misha choose capitulation or religious redemption? Hope or despair? The members of the audience are left to wonder and make their *own* choices.

Backstage, I had the good fortune to ponder the answer to the riddle with Elie Wiesel himself. Amazingly, the young actor playing the role of Misha in our production had a similar real-life dilemma: parents who rejected the past, grandparents who cherished it. His father had told him that having a bar mitzvah would be meaningless. The grandfather, a renowned star in American opera, had urged his grandson to claim the richness of his legacy. The boy had been confused for some time. But that night, after having experienced the emotions and arguments set forth in the play during rehearsal, the boy told me just before the curtain rose that he had made the decision to have a bar mitzvah and to claim his identity.

I will never forget the look on Elie Wiesel's face that night when I told him this story of hope that he had inspired with his poetic and powerful play. Tears brimming, his face shone as he gathered me in an embrace, whispering, "*Thank you. For this boy alone did I write this play. And now I know, finally, how the story ends.*"

Wiesel had created out of his wounds of loss and betrayal a work of art that could—and did—embrace the hope. To do so, he had to integrate the wisdom of his sorrow into the act of

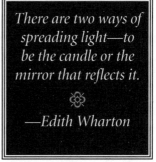

There are two ways of spreading light—to be the candle or the mirror that reflects it.

—*Edith Wharton*

writing. Wiesel generated an authentic sense of hope in his play by showing us that we must speak out, even in the face of fears and threats, if we are to create the possibility for hope in our fragile, lovely world. He inspired a young child to find meaning and purpose in his own consequential choice. Coming full circle, Wiesel, in turn, was blessed with the optimism he himself had set in motion.

Each one of us can lay claim to this hope by integrating the lessons of our healing and our higher consciousness and by allowing them to assist us in our unique work as artists of our own lives. We can fulfill our purpose only when we recognize, like Clare, that we are—wounds, wisdom, and all—*our own best destiny.*

———

THE TASK

As Clare did, we are going to create a *checklist of hope.*

Each day, record in your journal the images and feelings of hope you experience. You might recall the encouraging manner in which a coworker spoke to you, a friend's pregnancy, a card received from a grandchild or friend, a lover taking your hand.

Now add to this list specific acts *you* can perform, utilizing a knowing optimism, a hope based on the knowledge learned from your wounds. For example:

* Making a difficult decision based on what's best for your health and success rather than on what's convenient.
* Writing a letter to someone with whom you've had a disagreement or an estrangement; using a tone of healing rather than confrontation.
* Taking an hour with a family member or close friend for the sole purpose of helping them create a "checklist of hope."

Embracing the hope we draw from our Sacred Wounds can become a way of life. Make the most of it.

The Ritual

Meditate on the following folk legend. It concerns one group of people who learned nothing from their misfortune, and another that used their knowledge to forge hope, learning to succeed through integrating the lessons of their wounding experiences. This is a story about the difference between heaven and hell.

In hell there is a long banquet table brimming with food. The people sitting at the table are on high stools and their arms are wrapped in a snug material, cocoonlike. Each person holds his own solitary utensil, a four-foot-long spoon that he must wield with his mouth, making him unable to feed himself. The pain and suffering is everywhere.

In heaven's room, the set-up is exactly the same. A banquet table brimming with food. People, with arms wrapped snug and cocoonlike, sitting on stools with four-foot-long spoons that they wield with their mouths. Only here they are happy and well fed. How can this be? The difference is that here . . . they have learned to feed one another.

Close your eyes and guide yourself inward. Bless your ability to nourish a knowing optimism in yourself and others. Express in your heart that you love yourself enough to use the understanding and hope of your wounds to help you succeed on your life's journey.

The Gift

We affirm the actions we have taken and will take to integrate the lessons of our past wounds into who we are and how we act. These are the miracles of self-knowledge:

❀ I can take the lessons derived from my pain and use them as *emotional sunscreen* to protect me from negative influences while allowing the positive ones to flow into me.

❀ I can use the wisdom of my wounds to prompt me to make healthier and more positive *choices* that can lead me to the success I seek.

❀ Sacred Wounds help create a knowing optimism within me that fosters hope and keeps me on a journey surrounded by those who value the convictions of my heart.

> *Knowing is not enough; we must apply. Willing is not enough; we must do.*
>
> ✿
>
> —Goethe

❀ I can turn healing into hope when I am *mindful* of consciously moving myself forward through the steps of my journey.

❀ I am my own best destiny.

When we have taken *Step Seven* and embraced and integrated this hope forged from the understanding of our wounds, we have begun consciously activating the true power of our Sacred Wounds.

By affirming the optimism born of our ability to use our most painful lessons, we discover the blessings within our wounds.

It is these blessings that we will work to generate and receive, as our quest expands in *Step Eight* to embrace *spiritual success*.

STEP EIGHT

GENERATING THE BLESSINGS: Spiritual Power, Spiritual
Passion, Spiritual Purpose

If you would live happily, do not exaggerate life's evils,
nor slight her blessings.
—Joseph Joubert

THE MEDITATION

My journey in life is filled with meaning
for I choose to live it with purpose.
And now, raising my eyes,
a spiritual aurora emerges above me.
I stand unguarded under its canopy of light,
bathing in the energy of its illumination,
my life's intentions unfolding from my heart
in thanksgiving.

May I live fully in the luminescence of meaning
And freely in the radiance of purpose
Of all that I am
And have ever hoped to be.
Let me recognize the bounty in my living,
The gifts in my learning.
Help me to embrace the many blessings

Of where I've been—
where I am right now—
and where I am yet going. . . .

———

Just as the knowing optimism of our wounds can lead to a revolution in the way we live our lives, success is also to be found in the evolution of our spirit, the transformation of our soul. It is only now, after embracing hope as our road map, a hope based on the integration of knowledge derived from our pain, that we are ready to take *Step Eight*, where we will generate and receive a final tool that leads to empowerment and success. It is a tool, not of the heart or the mind, but of the spirit. It is the optimism grounded in experience that makes this step possible now, for it allows us to scale the heights along our journey that will give us the necessary vision by which we can attain the fulfillment of our quest. And it is only now that we come to define success fully, not only in the physical and emotional realm, but in the *spiritual* one as well.

Spiritual success speaks neither to our minds nor to our hearts, but to our souls. We may choose to use the terms *spirit, psyche,* or even *inner child,* rather than *soul*; they all refer to that which inhabits our essence. The soul is not corporeal in nature or emotional in substance. Rather, it is fashioned through the illumination of meaning. Science attempts to answer *how* the world came into being, *how* human beings function biologically as living creatures, *how* life evolves. The soul seeks to know *why.* Why are we here? Why do we suffer? Why do we seek healing and hope? We can say we've attained "spiritual success" when we're satisfied with our answers to these questions. Knowing why we're here, why life has purpose, gives the concept of success *transcendence.* It lifts success beyond the world of people, places, and things, and into the realm of spiritual power, spiritual passion, and spiritual purpose.

As we move through *Step Eight,* we embrace the concept of "spiritual success" as part of our definition of overall success, and recognize that our soul's success is integral to being fully alive. We come to this spiritual illumination not only by integrating the lessons of our painful experiences and fostering an attitude of knowing optimism, as we did in *Step Seven.* We attain this light of spiritual power, passion, and purpose when our Sacred Wounds generate blessings of insight out of that now-realized optimism, leading us to an understanding of why we are here, a question central to the truth of our life's destiny.

If we've ever had the gnawing feeling that we were meant to be doing more meaningful things with our lives, then we know what it is to have a soul in search of light. One of the ways this illumination enters our being is through the portals of pain created from the wounds we suffer. This pain influences our living conditions, and the choices we make. When we say that our wounds have taught us to seek out relationships that affirm our integrity, honor our feelings, embrace our hopes, we are speaking of emotional blessings that our hearts have received. When we say that our wounds have imbued us with a sense of direction, meaning, and hope, that we cannot settle for an existence that is anything less than fully alive, that our souls vibrate with a fullness that can only come when purpose and passion are in alignment, we are talking of spiritual blessings that our souls have received on our journey of *steps.*

THE LADDER OF LIGHT

*I*n the Book of Genesis, Jacob flees from his brother Esau after having tricked their father into giving him the blessing of the firstborn. Esau, stripped of his future inheritance as the eldest son, seeks his brother's life. Jacob, meanwhile, fears his brother's vengeance, and is deeply disturbed by his own actions. He knows he has cheated his brother and lied to his father, and these lacerations to his conscience torment him during his journey. As he lies down to sleep in the wilderness, far from home, he has a vivid and soul-shaking dream: he sees the spiritual image of a ladder stretching into the heavens, with myriad angels descending and ascending it. Jacob awakens with a sudden awareness that redemption is possible, and with the knowledge that, even in fear and anguish, "God was in this place and I knew it not." Jacob understands from his dream that his journey of heartache carries with it a spiritual purpose, for the opening within his soul caused by his own actions had allowed the light of blessing to enter. Years later, it is this *spiritual purposefulness* that brings him to face the sorrow he has caused when he asks his brother Esau for forgiveness. He may have been blessed by God, but his soul required more—the blessing of forgiveness only his brother could give.

So, too, can we come to the realization that the complete expression of our soul's aspirations can be made possible by sanctifying our life's hurtful and distressing experiences. We, *our truest selves*, are transformed when our wounds take root in our souls and create an awareness of spiritual illumination we never knew existed.

Like Jacob, we, too, have dreams. They exist as touchstones of spirit that animate and energize the direction we must take on our soul's quest for success. By reaching for that illumination, we climb the ladder of light raised by the higher consciousness coming from our wounds. This is a ladder of spiritual ascent, and as we ascend it we move, rung by rung, from the pain of our body and heart to the discovery of a spiritual power connected to the light of our wounds.

Our journey in life includes hardship and obstacles. This is the nature of any journey that involves forward motion into the unknown. Our soul interprets the glow of our Sacred Wounds as a lantern leading us to actions that can fulfill our higher purpose. Such purpose means looking at both the physical context of where and how we are living and also the spiritual context that defines *why* we are here. To speak of the evolution of our soul is to return to an encounter with the ladder of light, for our soul flourishes in the presence of illumination. As we look closer, we see that it is *we* who illuminate the ladder that is stretched between earth and Higher Possibilities. It is lit by our souls, *charged* with the energy of awareness, *electrified* with the surge of hope, *emblazoned* with the power of purpose.

Step Eight involves actively *seeking out* light and turning away from the darkness of negativity that can destroy our spiritual selves. It is the blessings generated by our Sacred Wounds that make possible this spiritual success, which is a precursor to our ultimate goal in attaining success for the whole of our life.

There is a remarkable event of nature that symbolizes how and from what source illumination can emerge. The aurora borealis, or northern lights, is an annual natural occurrence that draws observers from around the world to Alaska, Canada, Norway, and Finland. This precious and spectacular pathway of light, however, is not produced by gentle and tranquil phenomena. This gift of light is generated by particles sent into our atmosphere by violent solar storms, which are then charged and drawn by the magnetic pull of the North Pole. This cosmic pull and tug, the struggle of storms and resulting tension-charged particles, create this miracle, this awe-inspiring luminescence.

Our wounds perform a similar miracle. For it is in life's most traumatic tempests and struggles that sacredness and illumination are revealed to us. Such illumination is enhanced by our awareness of how our past injuries, emotional and spiritual, have shaped *who* we have become and *why* we make the life choices we do. The blessing of illumination becomes abundantly real when we are suddenly able to see how our negative choices and actions resulted from our wounds, and how they were responsible for inhibiting our growth and inflicting additional pain. At the same time, when we reach consciously for the light, we realize how profoundly we have grown and evolved as human and spiritual beings. Our soul glows with kindness, understanding, love, integrity, laughter, and hope. We *see* our journey now for all that it is—the redemption of the promise accompanying us when we came into this world to succeed at bringing forth our own unique light.

THE EIGHT RUNGS OF BLESSING

*T*o complete our quest for the empowerment that is *Step Nine*, we first must climb across a precipice. Some may call it a leap of faith, yet I see it not as a horizontal jump of religious abandon, but as a conscious *step up* to a clearer view of the spiritual blessings of our Sacred Wounds. There are eight rungs on this ladder of light that lead us up to the final leg of our quest. But like the Zen Buddhist koan we examined in *Step Five* in which enlightenment was found only *within* the experience, spiritual success is attained in the accumulated *experience* of the journey, not in any particular step along the way.

> *We are not human beings on a spiritual journey. We are spiritual beings on a human journey.*
>
> ⚜
>
> —*Stephen Covey*

Through our Sacred Wounds, our soul can find the light of its higher calling in spiritual power, spiritual passion, and spiritual purpose. It generates the certain awareness within our soul of why we are here in the world and on this journey. It is an awareness that will lead us to ultimate success. This is our blessing and our challenge: to climb each rung of the ladder of light every day of our lives.

The Eight Rungs of Blessing are:

Be aware always that we matter profoundly.

Live today's promise with fortitude and faith.

Elevate our purpose to embrace a higher calling.

Shine our soul's light on the best in ourselves.

Share the adventure of living with passion.

Illuminate life with the beacon of kindness.

Nourish our living with spiritual insight.

Grow deeper each day by acknowledging life's blessings.

Taking *Step Eight*, we embrace the Eight Rungs of Blessing as part of our journey. By choosing to make this ascent each day, we are also affirming our awareness that success carries with it a spiritual dimension. Like the aurora borealis, we reveal our truest selves in all our multihued and awesome light *because* of the *charged atmosphere of our soul*. It is our Sacred Wounds that not only generate this illumination of insight, but teach us how to grow into the light.

———

This is the story of a nun who had to make a life-changing decision based on the blessings of her Sacred Wounds. They were blessings that led her to discover "spiritual success" in the most unlikely of places.

Yvette's Story

Yvette had wanted to become a nun ever since she was a child growing up in a small town in Quebec in the 1940s. While others her age dreamed of becoming teachers, mothers, nurses, or actresses, Yvette felt a calling to God. Her mother was devoutly Catholic, and the family was extremely poor. Yvette was forced to work to help make ends meet while still in grade school. Her childhood was made even more painful as she witnessed her father's abuse of her mother, especially after he drank. Her home often felt like a war zone, and her two older brothers had fled the moment they entered their teens. In this setting, the Church had become a refuge and a home to Yvette. Even while she was still a teenager, she felt that she was meant for a higher purpose—and the Church offered her a path toward meeting that purpose.

As she grew into young womanhood, Yvette had not paid much attention to boys. But they certainly paid attention to her. With flowing raven hair, blue eyes that always seemed to catch the light, and a lithesome figure, Yvette drew attention no matter how shabby or out of style her clothes. And then there was the allure of her apparent unattainability. Although she took part in many school activities, including her role as soloist in the school chorus, Yvette was most drawn to the catechism retreats the area parishes held during school vacations. She particularly liked one of the leaders, Sister Agathe.

Sister Agathe, as they say, was "old school." She loved using music as a spiritual motivator, and really listened to the young people on her retreats, rather than treating them as errant sheep. Yvette soon became Sister Agathe's favorite, and their talks about God and the calling of a nun often lasted deep into the night. It was Sister Agathe who first broached the subject of the opposite sex, turning Yvette crimson with embarrassment. Sister Agathe brought it up because, well, there was this "problem."

The problem came in a male package, seventeen years old, six feet tall, with a thatch of red hair and a smile as big as the province. His name was Robert, and he had a serious crush on Yvette. Every day after school, he asked if he could walk her home. When she demurred, he made up excuses about having to go that way anyway even though she knew he lived far off in the opposite direction. Robert found time to talk with Yvette between classes, at church on Sunday—anytime he had a chance.

At first Yvette found it all a bit funny; then, little by little, she became angry and not a little confused. On the one hand, there was something in her that liked Robert's attention; sometimes she even found herself hoping he would show up. But, on the other, she knew this wasn't right. Someone who was going to give herself to Christ had no business dating—period. It wasn't fair to God, to Yvette, and especially not to Robert. Sister Agathe listened to Yvette talk about her "problem" and smiled. Perhaps she shouldn't be so quick to run away from her feelings, she suggested. Yvette disagreed.

It all came to a head on the night of Robert's senior dance. Bill Haley and Fats Domino were all the rage, but there was a new kid on the block who was challenging for the title of "King"—Elvis Presley. Yvette, despite her religious predilections and her parents' disapproval, loved his records. There was going to be a solid hour of Elvis records played at the senior dance, so Yvette finally accepted Robert's invitation for a date—"just to hear the music."

They stood by the wall of the gymnasium, listening to music and making small talk with Robert's friends for most of the evening. She was sixteen; the others were nearly eighteen. But she kept up her end of the conversation. When Elvis's ballad "Love Me Tender" started up, Robert finally convinced Yvette to try just one dance. Robert awkwardly took her hand, slipped an arm around her back, and together they shuffled side to side. Yvette began to feel sensations she had never known and became flushed as he pressed against her ever so slightly. And then, as the song was ending, Robert's feelings got the better of him. He held her close and then, before they parted, he kissed her. It was a small, delicate touching of lips, but it was real, and it left her trembling. Yvette stood back, blinking with incomprehension at what had just happened. Robert smiled at her hopefully. And then, from out of nowhere, Yvette slapped him. It was wrong, she told him, and furthermore he knew it. She wasn't going to be with boys. Not in that way. Hurt, confused, and shaking, Yvette left the dance and made sure she was never alone with Robert, or any boy for that matter, again.

As she headed for graduation during the next two years, Yvette confided in Sister Agathe her feelings about boys. The nun counseled Yvette to allow those feelings to materialize more fully. Celibacy was a major step, and it wasn't for everyone. People could serve God in all kinds of capacities, she reminded her. But Yvette was certain of her choices and had been for as long as she could remember. The thought of becoming a nun filled her with joy. She wasn't meant to be in a world in which husbands could beat wives and poverty was a badge of shame. Her purpose wasn't to work to scrape together money that her father could drink away. No. She was sure she was meant for God. Now, if only God were sure about her. Yvette was waiting for Him to speak to her, because her mother had promised that God would call her when He was ready. Sister Agathe couldn't argue with that.

Two years later, as her friends left for college or started new jobs, Yvette kissed her family good-bye, visited Sister Agathe once more, and then moved to the Convent of the Sisters of Notre Dame de Sacré Coeur, outside Montreal, to begin her formal training. Yvette went through the novice experience with all the enthusiasm of an eighteen-year-old finally entering a world she had always dreamed about. With the other novices, postulants, and nuns, she took turns scrubbing the stone floors, baking, cleaning the kitchen facilities, tending the garden, and taking classes in Catholicism and the history of her Order. She also joined the choir and read incessantly.

Yvette soon gained great favor among the nuns for her hard work, her thirst to learn, and her lovely voice, which lent musical beauty to daily prayer. Yvette could often be found in the garden or in a nearby woodland, still seeking the sign from God. Sister Agathe had said that she would know if and when God was taking her hand and calling her to service. It was a sign she searched for in prayer and in her training, but felt certain she would hear most easily in the cathedrals of nature.

When Yvette became a postulant, the step before taking final vows, she was just twenty. She had warmed to her role as a teacher in a local parish Sunday school, particularly because she felt for the first time what it was like to be really valued. The sisters encouraged her to take courses at a nearby college run by the diocese, which she did to her great enjoyment. Gone were the algebra, social studies, and home economics of her high school curriculum. Instead, she took high-level classes such as religious philosophy, classical history, and world anthropology. Yvette couldn't get enough; she felt as if she were breathing for the first time.

At the same time, Yvette was receiving instruction from the sisters in preparation for taking her vows. By the time she was in her mid-twenties, she had earned a degree in religious studies, and felt prepared to serve as a high school teacher wherever she might be sent. And still she sought out the Voice for her calling. It had become a wedge between her and the vows she longed to take. She was convinced that she would hear God tell her He needed her, not the other way around. One day she went to confession and admitted her growing sense of anxiety. And it was after five years at the convent, during that confession, that Yvette finally found an answer. It came in the person of a wise old priest who was a favorite in the convent. He was plain-spoken, had a good sense of humor, and was filled with the joy of service.

Father Rouberd had heard Yvette's anxious confession before, but this time he responded to an urgent sorrow that was pouring out from within her. She had always wanted to be a nun. She had been preparing for it ever since her mother first told her of the glories of serving Christ back when she was a little girl. There was an emptiness inside of her that she had sought to fill through religious service. But Sister Agathe had told her she would know in her soul when God had placed His mission and her destiny together. She craved the spiritual fulfillment she believed would come when He spoke to her. However, this had not happened yet. She had been led to believe she could not and should not take her final vows without such a sign. How long would she have to wait?

Father Rouberd's answer was brief and profound. "You know of your love and desire to serve God? Of this you are certain?" Yvette was in tears; of course she knew. "Well, then," the priest concluded, almost whispering. "Who do you think has placed such certainty within you if *not* God?" He paused, listening to her gentle sobbing. "Your answer is already in your heart. What are you waiting for, my child?" That was it. She would wait no longer.

Yvette was twenty-six when she took her final vows, and the sisterhood welcomed her with open arms. There was even talk that she could one day be elevated to head of her Order. The thought of becoming a mother superior secretly thrilled Yvette. Perhaps this would be her ultimate destiny after all.

The year was 1968. The Vietnam War was raging, men were escaping the draft into Canada, and Sister Yvette packed her bags to join a convent where she could both enjoy nature and teach at a wonderful new Catholic high school, St. Mary's, across the border in Vermont. Yvette loved the sisters of her new school. There were many who shared her infinite love of hiking in the woods, and she found particular satisfaction in her work with the students. The kids were somewhat rebellious; it was the challenge of authority that went with both their age and the times. But Yvette was most alive when teaching, connecting ideas with the young people in her class, helping foster their search for answers from God and the universe.

Sometimes, however, she would be vaguely dissatisfied, even after the most stimulating workdays. The emptiness Yvette had felt earlier in her life had subsided, but it had not disappeared entirely. Why was that, she wondered? If God had filled her life, if she had turned herself over to Him, how could there still be a void of any kind? Was there more to her life's purpose? Was she meant for another calling? These thoughts disturbed and frightened her. Her only answer was to drown her sense of spiritual failure in a sea of activity.

It was this continued search, however, that led her to feel particularly close to the students who were also on a spiritual quest. They fervently questioned the war, the drafting of boys their age, the assassinations of the Kennedy brothers and Martin Luther King, Jr., and sought to understand their meaning in the larger scheme of their lives. Were young men their age born to lose their lives in a rice paddy in Southeast Asia for a people and a cause they knew nothing about? If civil rights leaders and presidents could be gunned down in the streets, then where was God and why did He allow it to happen?

Several students incorporated their search for answers into the music they wrote and played at school assemblies—songs that not only protested the war in Southeast Asia, but also sought to articulate purpose in their own lives. Their music expressed their hearts' earnest desires. And it began to affect Yvette profoundly.

There was one young girl, Nancy, who reminded Yvette of herself at sixteen. She, too, was a singer. In addition, Nancy wrote folk songs on her guitar, songs that asked people to remember that they were all children of God. She sang of finding love rather than waging war. It was a cliché of flower-child philosophy, but it carried a spiritual dimension, Yvette thought. It was a sort of pop Catholicism, and Sister Yvette felt that if it gave the young people a ladder to God, the least God could do was meet them halfway. With the help of a local priest, she helped organize a "folk mass," a service that would feature the young people's music. Sister Yvette and some of her students placed dozens of candles around the altar and throughout the church, so it appeared as if the mass were taking place among the stars. The priest allowed the students to sing about their searching and their insights, and Nancy was the featured soloist. The priest then celebrated Communion with them as the benediction to their creative expression.

Yvette was thrilled to watch her students connect to God through their creative passion. After the mass she embraced each of them in turn, telling them how special they were. But where was Nancy? Yvette had to tell her how moved she had been by her song. She looked everywhere, to no avail. Perhaps the girl had already left for home? Coming out of the church, Yvette was headed for the parking lot when suddenly she saw a scene that stopped her in her tracks. Nancy was leaning up against a car engaged in a passionate kiss with one of Yvette's male students. Alarmed at first, Yvette stepped behind a birch tree. But she couldn't look away; she stood there, taking in with growing fascination the couple's unguarded passion.

Later that night in her room at the convent, Yvette thought back to that kiss on the dance floor with Robert. There was a stirring in her as she wondered about the feeling she had experienced then, and the feelings Nancy must have experienced in the parking lot. Over the next days and weeks, it was a question that seemed to grow in the deepest part of her, and it would not be easily dismissed by prayer, teaching, or the nun's habit.

Yvette sought out answers in the confessional, but the responses she received did little to quiet her heart. She found herself noticing with ever more intensity the intimate exchanges between her students after school by their lockers. When she would be having dinner at a restaurant or walking through town with the other nuns, she found her attention often wandering from their conversation. Instead, Yvette would find herself focusing on the touch of a man's hand on a woman's back as he held her chair in a restaurant, the passionate exchange of affection between a couple on a date, the laughter emanating from a husband and wife as they strolled hand in hand, children skipping all around them. This was not the world of her childhood. This was not the way things had been between her father and mother. She felt the sting of having watched the abusive relationship of her parents. The image of her drunken father filled her mind, and the sounds of slapping and the screams of her mother echoed within her. But in front of her was another kind of commitment and love that moved her completely. And the emptiness was felt not only in her heart, but most profoundly in her soul.

Finally, Yvette was impelled to confess her feelings to her mother superior. The kindly woman urged her to go on a retreat for thought and reflection. "There are many ways one can serve God," the nun counseled. Yvette thought back to Sister Agathe, who had expressed the same thoughts years earlier. It was she who had counseled Yvette not to close off the possibility that her calling lay elsewhere. Yvette could only see one path then. And now another one was forming in her soul, and its direction was overwhelming.

Yvette took a leave of absence from the convent and her teaching. She spent two weeks at a Catholic retreat center, and spoke daily with counselors of her growing concern about her celibacy and the sense that her soul seemed to be calling her to another destiny. It had shaken her faith and everything she had grown up believing about her mission in life. She had once been touted as mother superior material. Now she wondered at her commitment to being a nun. One counselor upset her by telling her that she had a kind of "buyer's remorse." Now that she had bought into the world of the sisters, he told her, something better would always be calling from around the next corner unless she matured and made her peace with God instead of fighting Him. Yvette didn't believe she had been fighting God. On the contrary, it felt to her as if she had been fighting herself.

It wasn't until Yvette spoke to Cynthia, another counselor, a former nun who had become a psychologist, that she began to glimpse the illumination that had been welling up within her. Cynthia and Yvette walked through the woods in the beautiful Green Mountains near Middlebury, Vermont, and talked for hours. Cynthia described her own quest for spiritual fulfillment, which had taken her into the Church and out again. She was still a Catholic, but found that life in the secular world was her true *spiritual* calling. How is that possible? Yvette wanted to know. "How could there be a higher spiritual calling than God?" She was bringing healing and direction to others, Cynthia explained, and at the same time she was able to explore her true love for God's creation through her commitment to another human being. Yvette found Cynthia's words both moving and liberating.

The next morning, Yvette went for a hike alone. It was here, in the cathedral of trees, where she had always felt most spiritually alive. As the sun filtered bright and golden through the branches, Yvette paused, taking in the canopy of illumination overhead. The truth had grown within her. Cynthia's words had unlocked what she already knew. Truly serving God meant being true to her own spirit, which was God's gift to her. She had never heard "the calling" but had allowed her spirit, wounded by the violence in her home that had shaped her views of love and sexuality, to push her into a life choice she had been convinced was her only avenue. She would have to follow her soul out into the world and rise to her higher purpose by exploring her own desire to give love to another.

Soon after, Yvette petitioned for release from her vows as a nun. She moved to Burlington and became involved in an educational foundation that served unwed mothers and others seeking to complete their education. There she met Craig, an exuberant educator and a lover of nature. The first time he put his arms around Yvette after a date, she began to tremble as she had years earlier when Robert had kissed her on the dance floor. Craig held her softly until the trembling subsided, and then kissed her with a passion she had never known.

That night Yvette shed tears of completion and wholeness. As their relationship grew, the wounds of her childhood, the void that had come from fear of intimacy and distrust of relationships, were replaced with spiritual completeness. She now found that a relationship between a man and a woman could be sacred. There was a light living within her now, reminding her how precious her life had become. When she and Craig married the next fall, Yvette knew that her soul was seeing the world with unprecedented clarity.

Yvette was finally right where she was supposed to be.

———

Yvette's journey led her to a series of insights that many people miss because they don't seek them. Our questioning, our unwillingness to settle, can elevate our spiritual existence as well as our physical one. By becoming aware of the emptiness in her soul and questioning it, Yvette opened herself to the possibility of taking another path. This path allowed her to fulfill her unique destiny by disproving a *core belief* she had held since childhood, a belief that told her that love between a man and a woman was necessarily violent and demeaning. By allowing herself to experience the empty space inside her, and by avoiding trying to fill it with alcohol, self-abuse, or anything other than her own truth, Yvette found her true destiny. This is not to say that those who choose a monastic life are not finding their higher purpose. Many of them most definitely are. I know priests, monks, and nuns who are truly fulfilled in their calling. But this was not Yvette's destiny. She could be most profoundly godly only when expressing her spirituality in her most profound human relationship.

By the way, she and Craig went on to have two children, both of whom can attest to Yvette having become a *superior mother.*

BECOMING WHOLE

*B*y recognizing that success includes paying full attention to our spiritual self as well as to our emotional and physical selves, we will accelerate the integration of all of our parts into a single, blessed whole. It is only in that state of completeness that we can truly know the success we seek. Ralph Waldo Emerson said the three most important things one can teach a child are *"to be kind, to be kind, and to be kind."* In sharing that attitude with the world around us, we elevate humanity, and we find in humanity's success a fulfillment of our own soul's purpose. When our soul comes to attain spiritual success, the light within the cup of our life not only "runneth over," it continually refills itself.

There is a Hebrew word with which many are familiar— *shalom.* It means both "hello" and "good-bye," but its fullest meaning can be seen when combined with the concept of *peace.* You greet people or take leave of them with the hope that they will come and go in peace. The root of this word is the Hebrew *shalem,* meaning "whole" or "complete." I interpret this as meaning that we can never have a sense of inner peace without a sense of being whole and complete. In order to accomplish this, we must come to embrace all facets of ourselves. That would, of course, include our soul.

This interpretation of the root of *shalom* also underscores what is at the core of Sacred Wounds—that success—physical, emotional, and spiritual success—involves embracing our wounds, for our sorrow and healing are essential parts of who we are. It is never just our body that is wounded. Being wounded is often physical, always emotional, and undeniably a *spiritual* experience. When we work to make *spiritual success* a part of our overall quest for success, then we are generating a blessing by making ourselves whole.

And when this occurs, we are blessed with the possibilities that come with inner truth and from knowing that we now embody spiritual power, passion, and purpose. It is this step that leads us to redeem the promise of our complete potential as a child of the universe.

———

THE TASK

Take time now to consider anew the Eight Rungs of Blessing (page 196) and incorporate the conscious life choices we need to take *Step Eight:*

In your journal, record your thoughts about how you might ascend each rung of this *ladder of light*. For example, ask yourself *how* you can increase your awareness that you matter profoundly. Is it by taking care of your own physical and spiritual needs? How specifically might this be accomplished? Do you need more time for yourself, more walks in nature like Yvette, more pampering of your spirit? Do you need to ensure that your thoughts and ideas are considered more seriously in any particular forum? Have you presented your ideas in a way that may have signaled that they and you don't matter?

Don't rush your answers. Do the same for each of the rungs until you have a firm idea of how you will incorporate this particular *step* into your life. Since each of us is unique, our journey up the ladder will be unique as well, leading to the unique blessing we can generate under the aura of our own illumination.

THE RITUAL

Spiritual success is not only a blessing born of our Sacred Wounds, it is a state of mind—or rather "a state of soul."

☞ Play some music, light a single candle in the dark, and meditate on the light of that single flame. Consider the blessings that have touched your spirit as you have taken the *eight steps* on this journey thus far. Recall each one, from *Acknowledging the Wound* to *Generating the Bless-*

ings. Envision the ladder of illumination that you yourself have fashioned from the light of your learning. That flame in front of you is connected to your spirit. Fill your soul with that light.

THE GIFT

You have a soul bursting with possibilities. The miracles of self-knowledge emerge when we see how our soul brings us closer to who we truly are.

Remember:

- ❁ We stand in the light of our Sacred Wounds, and *hear* the essence of *who we are* calling us to a higher purpose; this is an integral part of our quest for success.
- ❁ When we stand on the ladder of spiritual success, we are able to *see* our life's purpose with inner clarity.
- ❁ The soul is energized when we act on our inner truth. This creates a world in which we want to live, investing it with a profound purpose and meaning.
- ❁ We were meant to live in harmony with our soul's passion and power. To achieve this, we must pay attention to what our wounds can teach our spirit about the destiny we were meant to fulfill.
- ❁ We are not victims waiting for whatever tomorrow might throw at us, but rather conscious and conscientious shapers of our future. We can use our soul in this sculpting process, for the light within it tells us where we most want to go.

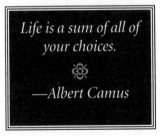

Life is a sum of all of your choices.

❁

—Albert Camus

We are our own best destiny. And that destiny will always include a *spiritual aurora* that illuminates the path we choose.

It is the blessing we receive when wounds are allowed to charge our spirit with the gift of light . . . and the gift of life.

Our *eight steps* have led us to our *ninth* and final one, where we will learn to claim *empowerment* from the spiritual step we've just taken. After integrating all aspects of ourselves into a whole, we move to *Step Nine,* where we will fully realize how the power and light from our wounds can transform our dreams into a blazing reality.

STEP NINE

TRANSFORMING POWER INTO EMPOWERMENT:
Breaking Through to the Life We Want

> *. . . and then the day came*
> *when the risk to remain tight in a bud*
> *was more painful than the risk it took to blossom.*
> —Anaïs Nin

THE MEDITATION
There is a positive energy that is mine alone.
It radiates through my mind, my heart, and my soul.
May I use its gifts and blessings to realize my dreams
And those aspirations that live within me.

This power is born of the wounds of my experience,
Elevating me and enlarging my vision.
Their light now courses through me,
imbuing me with purpose.

May I use these Sacred Wounds
To move me forward on the arc of success
And make a difference in the world.

For I am a rainbow of mobility
painted with my own colors,
pouring forth across the canvas of life.

I alone can empower my future,
And I embrace that opportunity
With all my life and all my spirit.

It is a celebration of all that I am and will yet be.

———

How do we break through to the life we want? The eight previous *steps* have helped us gradually to convert our sorrow to wisdom, clarity, hope, and spiritual illumination. It has happened *because* of life's pain. Before moving on, let's pause to appreciate our journey through the discovery and blessings of our Sacred Wounds:

- In *Step One,* we learned how to acknowledge the suffering that has invaded our lives and to recognize our pain in order to awaken a newfound consciousness within us. Like Debrah, we have seen how our sorrow can open our eyes to new avenues of integrity and empathetic intelligence when we hear *the voice of our wound.*
- *Step Two* showed us the debilitating effects that unexamined and unchecked traumas can have on us, particularly when they are fueled by *guilt* and *self-blame.* Like Brad, we discovered that corrosive guilt can keep us imprisoned in *cycle wounds* that inflict us repeatedly and cause us to make destructive, sabotaging choices over and over again. By *letting go of the guilt,* we learn that we hold the key to the *kingdom of healing.*
- In *Step Three,* we saw that when we *drain the profane* elements of our injuries, we are liberated from the contamination of negative internal messages. Like Lena, we see that our *core beliefs,* based on the initial experience of our anguish, limit and even damage how we think about ourselves and the world. We can replace these limiting

thoughts, however, with *alternative beliefs* that emphasize forgiveness, self-love, and inner strength and give us the power to envision a more affirmative path as we go *in search of the sacred.*

❀ In *Step Four*, we found that when we *accept the wisdom of our wounds*, we can transform pain into possibility, bringing us forth from grief and loss to the birth of the *sacred* within us. It is this sacred awareness and knowledge that is our *life-right.* Like Rick and Sara, we found that if we *reframe* challenges in life and downsize previous obstacles we can then discover in this *silver cloud* opportunities for self-growth.

❀ It is this finely tuned sense of purpose that moved us to *Step Five*, where we learned to recognize the signposts pointing to the true journey that our wounds have offered us, however invisible it once may have been. Here we uncover this *precious path* toward our heroic quest for meaning and the surprising successes it can produce. Like Steve, we found that once we drop our illusions of a perfect life and accept the essential imperfections of existence, we are free to recognize our capacity for joy, and embrace it more fully *because* we have been wounded. This newfound direction grants us a clarity to see what is truly meaningful in life and to expel the trivial and damaging pressures. Only then can we gain an unobstructed view of the success we so passionately seek.

❀ In *Step Six*, we saw that when we accept and *honor our wounds*, we can recognize those angels among us and within us urging us to "*Grow, grow.*" We find that our pain has opened us to a higher consciousness, where empathy and compassion infuse us with *purposeful living.* Like Kurt, we discovered that honoring the experience of our grief and sorrow reveals the grief and sorrow of others; this, in turn, inspires us to reach out beyond the defensive walls we may have built and help to bring comfort and renewal into the world. Now we can see that *we* choose to concentrate either on ugliness and limitations or beauty and affirmation.

- The ability to choose affirmation moved us to *Step Seven,* where we learned to embrace hope forged from the understanding produced by our wounds. It is this *knowing optimism* that proves to be the road map that keeps us true to our journey. Being *mindful* of how our pain has woven its wisdom into our feelings can serve as an *emotional sunscreen*, keeping out external destructive messages while allowing in those that affirm our purpose. We can prompt ourselves to make choices that give us a new and fuller commitment to following our life's compass. Like Clare, we found that learning the lessons of our wounds allows us to embrace a living "checklist of hope" that can, in turn, inspire us to discover that we are our own best destiny.
- It is this purposeful living combined with an energized optimism that propelled us ahead to *Step Eight*. It was only at that point in our journey that we were able to complete our definition of success; we noted that success is achieved not only through physical and emotional happiness, but through *spiritual* fulfillment as well. Like Yvette, we came to understand that the soul's ability to be charged with spiritual vision is made possible by the light within our Sacred Wounds. By climbing a ladder of light provided us *because* of our suffering, we claim a wholeness of spirit we have never known. The glow of our "completeness" generates further blessings of insight as to why we are here and the redemption of the unique promise of our existence. This illumination infuses our quest for success with a spiritual power.

Now armed with these insights and wisdoms, we are ready to take *Step Nine*. Here we will learn to break through to the life we want, by *empowerment*.

THE QUEST FOR EMPOWERMENT

*D*r. Abraham Joshua Heschel was rescued from the horror of the Holocaust and brought to America to teach. He became one of the greatest spiritual philosophers of the twentieth century, inspiring Jews, Muslims, Buddhists, Hindus, and Christians alike. Heschel said: "To be or not to be is NOT the question—rather it is HOW to be and how NOT to be." Part of this step toward empowerment comes from learning from our Sacred Wounds *how* and how *not* to live our lives, so that we are not only capable of success— but are *worthy* of it as well.

Vision:
the art of seeing
things invisible.

—Jonathan Swift

The renewed vision of our unique purpose in life has clarified and elevated our priorities and our direction. As we have seen, Sacred Wounds teach us how to distinguish between what is truly important and what is trivial in our lives. By bringing that wisdom to bear on the present, we empower ourselves to transform dreams into reality and our past pain into today's personal triumph.

George Bernard Shaw once observed that "life isn't about finding yourself. Life is about creating yourself." We have been doing exactly that by taking such an active role in re-creating ourselves. In essence, *we are the midwives of our own rebirth*.

Step Nine—attaining empowerment—is accomplished when we have been reborn as a fully formed human traveler; it happens when we embody the gifts of wisdom, honor, love, hope, purpose, blessings, and wholeness imparted by our life's Sacred Wounds.

Up until now we could not unleash our full inner power

because that power resides in the very Sacred Wounds that await our gaze and acceptance. But now we have integrated the physical, emotional, and spiritual aspects of ourselves. We have embraced the lessons of our pain that are integral to our life's success. Now we are whole, for we have integrated our sacred wounding into our full selves. We stand now on *sacred* soil, on the crest of our journey, ready to take up the *empowerment* that we have sought.

What is empowerment? It is true self-actualization, that which enables us to realize our highest potential. Empowerment is a force within us that comes from our possession of wisdom, hope, clarity of vision, and spiritual illumination, but, even more so, infuses us with the certain knowledge that we are able to activate that power to accomplish our life's purpose and make manifest our dreams.

How shall we transform this power within us? By proving that we are now ready and worthy of wielding it.

THE PINNACLE OF THE QUEST

The connection between "worth" and a successful quest has been explored in scores of ancient myths and narratives. In the Arthurian legend Percival and the Quest for the Holy Grail, a wounded King Arthur languishes in pain as his kingdom, Camelot, slowly turns into a wasteland. The knight Percival goes in search of the Grail, the mystical cup of Christ, for it is said that once the Grail is found the king will be healed. During his quest Percival comes to understand the sacred connection between the king and his kingdom. The success of the land, he learns, is profoundly dependent on the health of the king. When Arthur's powers are diminished, the land loses its fertility and thus its ability to produce.

Percival realizes that if he is to claim the Grail, he must prove that he is worthy of it. In order to achieve the wisdom and experience that will enable him to do this, he must go out into a violent and bitter world and endure the suffering and sorrow that is found there. It is only after achieving the knowledge and understanding that accompany the grief and pain of a life honestly led that Percival finally gains the experience needed to win success. Proving worthy of the Grail, he heals the king, and the land is restored to its fecund and productive glory.

Like Percival's, our quest has taken us on a journey of *endurance* and *discovery*, where we can claim the *empowerment* we have earned. It is the Grail of this empowerment that will help us to break through to the life we want. Like Percival, *we* have been tried in a challenging and changing world and have suffered pain. We have also found that this pain fosters enlightenment if we are open to it. Like Percival, however, we must now prove our worth. In the myth, the knight discovers that the proof of his own worth came not from those he met, or from his fellow knights, or even from the king. It was found solely within his own heart. Once he had recognized that truth, he could then, and *only* then, succeed in his quest.

In order to bring our quest to its ultimate pinnacle of success and claim empowerment, we, too, must prove our worth. In the past, the success we desired may have gone unachieved because we had not yet learned from our Sacred Wounds. Our dreams were left unrealized, perhaps even unimagined, because an essential part of our personal power was left unclaimed and unused. Now we recognize that our worth is not established for us by our parents, our children, our spouses or siblings, our colleagues, or our friends. Our worthiness to claim empowerment is not granted by science, celestial signals, physical trainers or God. The proof of our worth can be found solely within ourselves. *It is in knowing our own worth and believing in our essential goodness that we transform power into empowerment.*

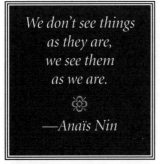

*We don't see things
as they are,
we see them
as we are.*

—Anaïs Nin

THE PATH IS OURS TO CHOOSE

A Hindu principle teaches that "truth is one, paths are many." In our nine-step journey we have sought not only truth, but the sacred path that is ours to lead. We have spoken of creating a life of higher purpose. We have seen our ideas of success grow to include physical, emotional, and spiritual dimensions. We must choose now to do the things that fulfill us and bring us happiness and meaning.

I once had the great honor to introduce a remarkable fifteen-year-old girl, Rachel, to a Los Angeles junior high audience. Clad comforably in jeans and a high school sweatshirt, her long black hair braided and held by a golden bow, Rachel stood quietly, looking out at several hundred young people her age who hadn't the slightest idea of the powerful gift she was about to give them. Taking a deep breath, she looked over at her mother in the first row, and then began:

"I'd like you all to close your eyes," she said. Everyone I could see complied, anticipating a fun and relaxing exercise. "Now imagine yourself waking up one morning after a terrific sleepover with your friends. Got that image in your head, okay? Use your imagination; I want you to really see yourself, your friends, and smell breakfast cooking. Suddenly, you're aware of a tingling sensation that has begun in your feet. Maybe you slept on something, and the circulation was cut off and you figure it'll pass . . . only it doesn't." The teens were shifting a bit, some began to open their eyes to look at Rachel. What was this all about? "Close your eyes, please," she urged. "We're on a journey together, only I want you to make it your own." As far as I could see, every one of the kids went along.

Rachel continued. "This odd tingling, you notice the next day, has spread to your legs and is slowly moving upward. Imagine it, feel your legs tingling, hear the sound of your heartbeat racing 'cause you don't know what's happening. Now you're scared, and your parents take you to the doctor, and she doesn't know what it is, so they take you to another doctor, who sends you to a specialist. Pretty soon you're on a medical merry-go-round, and no one knows what's wrong with you. Then—now really try to picture what this is like—your vision becomes blurred almost all the time."

Rachel paused, and asked, "Do you have that all in your mind?" The audience kept their collective eyes shut, and the room was hushed with attention. "Now imagine that you finally find a doctor who tells you he knows what it is—you've got multiple sclerosis. And you're both scared and relieved at the same time because now you know. And now you and your family can begin to deal with it." She paused, looking out across the sea of faces. "Open up your eyes now. That story was my story. I have MS."

Rachel described the feelings of loss and fear she had following her diagnosis. She described the road that had taken her from fear and anger to acceptance of the gifts that went with her condition: "Gifts so simple as feeling the sand on your toes. Don't ever take that for granted," she urged her listeners.

We ended the assembly with a question I had for her. I wanted to know if her MS had empowered her in any way. Rachel didn't hesitate for a minute. "I am so grateful to the MS for making me realize all that life has to offer and all I can be as a person. I wouldn't want it taken from me if it would mean that I wouldn't have had the experience of it to teach me that I am worth every success I create and that life is beautiful and precious every day."

Rachel had come to know a truth that was emphasized in many different ways on our nine-step journey: *we don't get to choose the pain that will come our way in life. But we do get to choose what that pain is going to mean.* It all comes down to the path we want for ourselves. We are that powerful and that empowered.

In fact, we are our own best power station. We *can* break through to the life we want, shaped by our vision, our optimism, our wisdom, and the blessings of a soul on fire. We are worthy of having it all! It is in our certainty of that self-worth that our power is transformed into empowerment and success becomes as sure as our ability to dream.

———

In the Introduction, I recounted the personal moment when my deepest wound was born—the day my children were told their mother was leaving our marriage and our home. Let me now come full circle to share with you my gradual journey from being a man with a wound to a man with a Sacred Wound, and how my life has been transformed by this rebirth.

Jan's Story

*D*uring the years when I raised my children as a single parent with primary physical custody, I had secretly, and with painful constancy, blamed myself for having failed to maintain a mother's presence in our house. The fact that my children's mother, my ex-wife, *chose* to leave was not in question, and I am in no way casting blame. She remained an important presence in their lives, spending time with them regularly and loving them always, but we just could not remain an intact family. The primary home in which my children grew from the ages of six, nine, and eleven to adulthood had been forever changed. For me, it was a home reeling from its wounds, searching for its footing, fearing for the future.

Soon after my wife's departure, I overheard my nine-year-old daughter speak words that broke my heart: "He's not only our daddy," she told her six-year-old brother as she tried to explain the new structure in our home, "he's our mommy, too." How had our lives been turned so completely upside down? How would the children ever cope?

While learning to do as much as possible to make up for my failings, I tormented myself, mostly at night when I was alone. I simply could not—*would* not—forgive myself. As time went on, we gradually became a new kind of family. Yaffa and Batsheva, my two daughters, and my son, Elisha, were truly astounding souls—and like most children they were far more resilient than I had expected. Every Wednesday evening, and on Saturdays, I would drive the kids to their mom's house, but this act of bringing them together (which I might have interpreted as a positive step) only underscored for me the void that was in my own home. Although I vaulted back and forth from anger to depression to determination to hope, I couldn't fully land in a positive, life-affirming place, because I still privately harbored and nurtured a wound that darkened from the messages I sent myself: I was not *good enough* or *worthy enough* to fill this role. Yes, I was proud of the father I had become. But it wasn't sufficient for me. Worse, it wasn't sufficient for *them*. I had somehow let my children down terribly, and wondered if they would ever believe in their own potential if their father couldn't fulfill his.

I managed to function with this sense of unworthiness while also finding the blessings in single fatherhood. With the dinners and carpools and after-school activities, I tried to become somebody my children could be proud of. We sang loud and often. Our theater games and family hugs, the big kisses and family celebrations, all brought us a joy and meaning that, particularly after having been wounded, mattered profoundly. The cooking and schlepping wasn't anything any single mom with primary custody of her children wasn't also expected to do. In 1982, all single parents faced the same challenge: how to foster an atmosphere in which children could learn to believe in themselves without the "necessary" two parents living together in the same home. My guiding quest was to protect my children so that they might blossom even though our home might be "different"; that quest defined the next thirteen years of my life. A decade after my youngest left for college I found my way into the offices of a trusted therapist, Steve, who had helped me years earlier cope with the pain of divorce and the challenges of sudden single fatherhood.

I walked into Steve's intimate, wood-paneled office near UCLA, and told him about my unfinished business. "I feel I was able to cope all these years," I explained. "And it's given me a lot of joy to see my children grow into such amazing adults. But . . ." I wasn't even sure how to phrase it. Steve nodded with a smile. "Take your time. It's all right."

The tears began to well up as I spoke what was in my heart: "At first, I got so I felt like I had discovered this power in me, that maybe I could do anything. Making breakfast for twenty-five eight-year-olds will do that for you." I chuckled. So did Steve. I bit my lip and continued. "Only it's like I need someone to tell me that it was all right, that all I did was enough. If I let my children down, if I couldn't even keep an intact home, I mean, what kind of success is that for a man?" I began to cry. Clearly it was much bigger an issue than even I had figured.

Steve thought for a minute, gathered his thoughts, then looked up with a hopeful smile. "You want to try something new?" he asked. "It's a new therapeutic technique I've just trained in called EMDR—Eye Movement Desensitization and Reprocess-ing." I look at him, puzzled. Was I so bad off that I needed a whole new therapeutic technique? Steve continued. "It's an accelerated form of therapy. The thinking is that it simulates the REM of sleep in which the mind gets in touch with images and feelings that we might not reach otherwise. I don't fully understand how it works, but I've seen it have surprisingly effective results. What could it hurt? You want to try? I think it could help you."

I asked about how I should prepare for a thing like this. Was there special equipment? Would I be lying down, or standing, or what? Steve calmed me with his gentle smile. "No, nothing like that," he said. "You just sit here, you'll follow movement back and forth, and then we'll tap into your memories. It's a journey we'll take together." Steve's enthusiasm for the EMDR encouraged me, and we scheduled a double session in order to provide time for its fullest and most potent effects.

I will say right up front that I suspected the whole thing was a little outlandish. How could simulating the eye movements we experienced when asleep do anything about the emotional trauma I harbored? On the day the therapy began I got there a little earlier than usual. Slowly I climbed the steps to Steve's office, took a deep breath, exhaled and said, "Here goes nothing." Steve invited me in, looking relaxed and confident. He led me to a soft leather chair, and pulled out what appeared to be a conductor's baton or a magician's wand. It was a thin, silver, two-foot-long telescoping pointer. Sitting opposite me, Steve told me not to move my head, but simply to follow the wand with my eyes as he flicked it from side to side. For about a minute he moved it metronome-style before my eyes. It had the feel of a hocus-pocus experiment, and I began feeling self-conscious and embarrassed.

After the first minute of nonstop movement, Steve stopped and asked me to tell him what I was seeing in my mind's eye. I described my children, how they'd done in school, how tall they'd grown, who was dating whom. After about thirty seconds he began moving the wand from side to side again for another minute; then he stopped, again asking me what I was feeling, seeing, sensing. After yet another minute I began shifting in my chair, because although I was skeptical about this technique, I was also aware that my responses to Steve's questions were becoming surprisingly vivid and emotionally powerful. Suddenly, Steve's questions were coming faster, almost blurring into the flurry of my eye movements. What was going on here?!

And then it happened, and to this day neither Steve nor I know exactly how. It seemed to grow in front of our eyes, and I was both inside myself experiencing the technique, and outside myself bearing witness to its effect.

I remember being suddenly present at the moment my wife informed the children of her decision to leave. It was February 15, the day after Valentine's Day. We had decided to tell them during a weekend, when they were free of school worries. In front of me, I could see with a startling power the children as they were that day. Every detail was crystal clear: I could sense my middle daughter to my right on the blue couch, my eldest daughter sitting to the left of me, and my young son bobbing around to the left of us, unable to sit still during his mother's difficult announcement of the painful changes in all of our lives. It was late in the morning, and the sun was filtering through the glass windows.

Then the scene changed abruptly; as Steve's questions, combined with my rapid eye movements, sparked images, events, even smells I had never before experienced. And it was terrifying.

I was on a battlefield. I could smell the sulfur of weapons discharging, and hear the sound of bullets and explosions in the distance. As the smoke of combat lifted, I could make out my three children in the near distance. They seemed to be victims on this battlefield, dodging and running from the incoming attack. I was filled with a horror that nearly stopped my breath as I began running, attempting to reach them and shield them from the onslaught. But something was wrong. My feet weren't working right. It was like a film reel in slow motion, each step I took was painstakingly drawn out as I witnessed a hail of bullets heading toward my children. I could hear their screaming and even my own voice crying out to someone, anyone, to stop this madness. I was helpless to end it. The smoke was obliterating my view again, and the acrid odor of guns discharging filled my nostrils. I was unable to extricate myself from the emotional trauma of the scene before me, and I hated myself for my weakness, for not being able to throw myself in front of the hail of bullets coming my children's way.

I was aware that I was in Steve's office; I could even sense the colors of the rug beneath me, and the hum of the air conditioner. But in my mind's eye, aided by senses that were inexplicably intensified, I was on that battlefield, and the carnage was as real as anything I have ever known.

And then I heard Steve's voice asking me, "Where are you now?" and in an instant, the scene changed again.

I was in the wilderness. There was a mountain right in front of me; a strong, warm wind whipped around me, kicking up dust or sand that obscured my vision. I heard Steve telling me to concentrate on my visions and allow my pain free rein over my imagination. I didn't need his encouragement. I was already there. As the wind died down, I saw before me a scene that shook me to my core. Even in my mind's eye, I had to step back to take it all in, so frightening were the images.

Somehow, I was standing on Mount Moriah in Jerusalem, the site where Abraham was asked to sacrifice Isaac. I saw above me three donkeys being driven up a trail in the mountain bearing heavy provisions. As I drew closer, I saw on the backs of the donkeys not provisions but people, bound and helpless. And then I literally rose to my feet.

As I broke into a run and drew close to these figures, I saw a man wielding a knife as he drove the animals and their human cargo forward. And I realized with horror the identity of those figures—they were my children, whose innocence and lives were to be offered up on that altar, a sacrifice to an unfeeling God. With my fists clenched and tears streaming down my face, I experienced all over again the terror and fear of violence threatening my three beloved children.

As I raced to catch up with them, I feared I would once again be too late. Again they would suffer their wounds, and again I would be powerless to stop it from happening. At that moment, however, I experienced yet another change in scene. In my vision, I was atop the mountain now. I was above this nameless individual with the knife, facing him as he was about to place my eldest on the altar. Suddenly, I was upon this man, wrestling with him, straining with every ounce of strength to rescue my children's lives . . . and my own.

I heard Steve's voice, and tried to pull away and hear what he was saying, but I was in the midst of this terrifying struggle and was having difficulty hearing him. Then, however, I heard Steve asking me to stop and look over to the side of my vision. "What can you see there, Jan? Anything?" he asked. "Look over, look over now." With tremendous effort, I paused in my unyielding terror and fear. Trembling, I turned my head from this scene of sacrifice and glimpsed something quite different and wondrous. A sudden calm came over me. In a surge of energy coming from my terror, I felt the emergence of a newfound empowerment.

To the side of my vision I saw my children. I smiled at them and told Steve what I was witnessing. He asked gently, "How are they doing?" I took in the moment as if it were a lifetime. They were standing there, smiling back at me. Each one was intact, alive, strong, and beautiful! I answered in a grateful gasp, "They are fine. Yes, they are safe. My God, they are okay."

The trauma I had felt, the powerlessness to protect my children from suffering, the failure I experienced in failing to give my children a home without pain, my sense that they were victims and it was my fault—all of this was the cornerstone of my sense of unworthiness. I wasn't good enough. But now I felt a deep and abiding knowledge that I was worthy after all. And this feeling empowered me with the conviction that I could do anything. And it was glorious and life-affirming, and I shook with the joy of it.

Steve listened as I made these connections myself, and when I was done, he sat quietly with me before asking a simple and gentle question: "What is *your* blessing?"

And my answers were suddenly as clear as the wound that had led me here. My gifts were many: I had been given the opportunity to raise my children in our home. I had been given the opportunity not to stop the pain (which was inevitable), but to use it to find power and purpose in our life as a family. We had grown together and been strengthened by the amazing knowledge that we could make our lives work. By going on with our lives, creating new family customs, and celebrating with songs and theater games and deep hugs and much love, I had helped my children and myself to move from a sense of helplessness to a state of hopefulness, to convert a sorrowful guilty energy into the power of love, hope, and joy, and to empower us to a life of celebration and of meaning.

In that moment, I found the empowerment of my Sacred Wounds. I stood in Steve's office literally embracing myself, overwhelmed by the clarity and the fullness of this new meaning. Steve looked at me with tears in his eyes. I asked Steve why he thought I had this vision of wrestling with the man on Mount Moriah; he laughed. "Your vision went from Abraham to another powerful story—Jacob wrestling with the angel. He was wounded, but he succeeded. And he was blessed. Just like you," he said. I laughed, still marveling at the intensity and relieved at the outcome. "I'm lucky you aren't a carpenter," Steve joked as we hugged each other good-bye. "We'd have been dealing with images of flying two-by-fours. Go home, live and love yourself. Amen."

On my way home I felt a little like Scrooge, having undergone a transformation all in one visit. But as I pondered the miracle of it, it occurred to me that my wound had been teaching me life lessons for some time. It had now finally liberated me, by revealing the truth about the messages of unworthiness I had been sending myself. I *was* enough for my children in our home; I had been all along. I had been allowed to both help create and take part in the success of my family. I had used my inner power to let my children know they were loved, and that they should believe in themselves as completely and unconditionally as I believed in them.

That day I became empowered with a sense of worth that had been out of my reach but which had, of course, been there all along. My wounds—my Sacred Wounds—had taught me that I not only could handle the lightning bolts of life's most traumatic experiences, but that the suffering itself had led me to elevate my own life as a man and a father. I was only now fully realizing the extent of that empowerment.

I vividly remember returning home after this therapy session. I had been living alone, but my son, Elisha, was visiting from college, and he was waiting for me when I opened the door. The excitement and power of my experience poured out as I shared with him all I had just seen, felt, and come to celebrate. Elisha looked at me with shining eyes and a warm smile. When I finished the tale, he rose up and enveloped me in the embrace of a lifetime. "Good for you, Dad," he said, holding me tightly. "Good for you."

And Elisha's hug itself felt like a benediction.

————

Simply put, I would never have become the father or person I am today without my sometimes bitter, sometimes traumatic life experiences. I came to recognize that success evolves (and can be learned) *because* of the shaping power of our Sacred Wounds. Although they can be unpredictable, painful, frightening, Sacred Wounds are also empowered and empowering! I would not have asked for them to be visited upon me, to be sure. I would have preferred that my children not experience pain and the loss of innocence so early in their lives. But we don't get to choose the pain life places before us. We only get to choose whether we will allow it to fester and relegate us to a *profane* existence, or whether we will accept and learn from it, using our wounds to empower us.

How do I know if the energy of my wounds transformed my life, and through me, the lives of others? Elisha was six years old at the time of the initial wound I've shared with you. He is now twenty-seven. Last Father's Day I received a hand-painted card from him. On the cover, a blazing figure, bearing some resemblance to my son, is lifting his arms up through the clouds, past the stars and onward. Inside he writes a message I will treasure all of my days:

> *You've taught this Golden Firechild*
> *that the sky is* not *the limit,*
> *to reach* beyond *the stars,*
> *to a place where dreams exist*
> *and are very real.*

That is proof enough of the empowerment of my Sacred Wounds, I suppose. But there is something more: they are what inspired, elevated, and propelled me forward to write this book and share it with you with heartfelt blessings.

We are transformed from victim to victor in the crucible of the Sacred Wound. The triumph blazes forth in the empowerment and optimism to be found in our daily approach to living. It is found in the success we can now create with the fullness of our worth.

———

THE TASK

In your journal, complete the following *empowerment prompts* with specific goals:

- ❀ The three things I want to do to elevate my life in the next three months are:
- ❀ I *can* take the following steps to get there:
- ❀ The three things I want to accomplish most in the next year are:
- ❀ I *can* do this by using the gifts that lead to my own empowerment. I will activate that empowerment by taking the following concrete steps:

Still round the corner there may wait a new road or a secret gate.

❀

—*J.R.R. Tolkien*

You *can* accomplish all of this and more. Nothing is written in stone. We are made of flesh and blood, hope and spirit. Allow for the freedom of your own aspirations. Know that the steps you will take to fulfill them are giant leaps on your journey to success.

THE RITUAL

Let us bring to completion the *sacred* circle of our time together during this journey of affirmation. Go to a place of solitude where you will not be disturbed for half an hour. We will share in a guided imagery meditation that will allow our quest to find full expression.

- ❀ Relax in a location of gentleness and light; allow yourself the freedom to simply *be*. Breathe deeply. Pay attention to the fullness of your breath and the completeness of exhalation. If emotions well up as you progress through this meditation, let them. They are an expression of who you are at this juncture in your life's journey. They are a celebration of who you are and where you've been.

⚜ Imagine now in the fields of your heart the faces of all of those, living and dead, who love and care about you.

⚜ Look at each one in turn, slowly. Study their faces. They are smiling, at peace with you. Look into their eyes, each one in turn. Feel the love they offer.

⚜ Let them softly and gently place their hands on you, on your back, your face, your hands, blessing you with their touch. It is the touch of *healing*. Allow yourself to receive that healing touch, feel it in your core, let it move you with its touch on your skin and in the depth of your emotions.

⚜ Now allow your cherished ones to move their gentle hands through your body, reaching deep within you, to your Sacred Wounds. Let them linger there and hold you with compassion at the center of the pain you have suffered. Their love is the love of healing; their touch is the touch of pure hope. Hold on to this moment. Then store these offerings of loving energy in your heart and soul.

⚜ Your loved ones bless you once more. Then, cradling your spirit with love, they drift into your heart. Feel the fullness within you. Cross your arms, embracing yourself, and with the gratitude for all you have achieved, express thanks to yourself for this empowering journey.

The Gift

We will use the self-knowledge we have acquired from each of our *nine steps* to create a guideline and a series of affirmations that celebrate the end of our quest to find empowerment in our Sacred Wounds.

In that spirit, we now weave together miracles of self-knowledge into a single *Manifesto for Success*. In composing it, let us recognize that it is a *living document*. As we continue our jour-

We make a living by what we get, but we make a life by what we give.

—Winston Churchill

ney, each of us will add to it in our unique way, based on our own life experiences.

A manifesto is a document of declaration. We direct it toward our minds, hearts, and souls. Share it with family and friends. Send it into the world by e-mail, include it in holiday cards, post it at work or on the refrigerator. However you choose, share this celebration of what is purposeful and possible in laying claim to our *sacred, illuminating, and empowering wounds.*

Let us turn now to the epilogue—our ending and our new beginning.

Epilogue

Manifesto for Success

I Am/I Will

I am the author of my dreams. I will not lose them to despair.

I am the builder of my tomorrows. I will not dwell in the collapsed imaginings of my yesterdays.

I am the wings of my aspirations. I will not be grounded by disappointment.

I am whole and unique. I will not devalue my self-worth.

I am choosing to let go of the guilt and the blame that keep me anchored in the past.

I will replace the core beliefs that prevent me from achieving my potential.

I am choosing today to accept the wisdom of life's woundings.

I will use the wisdom I've earned by my struggles to light my path to success.

I am choosing to recognize that I have a role in tipping the balance for good in the world.

I will seek out and celebrate the bonds that affirm our common, shared humanity.

I am able to recognize the choices that diminish my dignity.

I will count myself a success whenever I make choices that nourish my soul.

I am able to live a purposeful life by being true to my values.

I will use my life's experiences to transform my life with blessing.

I am able to live my own truth rather than follow the wavering standard of popular sentiment.

I will see in any failure the opportunity to learn.

I am able to hear the angels in my life, those around and within me, and I will heed their call always to grow.

I will embrace daily the illumination of my own spirit.

I am the recipient of life-rights that have been earned through my experience.

I will integrate these teachings into my vision of all I want my life to be.

I am choosing hope as my companion, optimism as my guide.

I will refuse to accept that which devalues my dreams.

I am choosing to live in the present while finding the gifts the past can teach me.

I will celebrate the life-force that sings within me.

I am choosing success as a way of life.

I will embrace my success with the power of my own goodness.

Because knowing who I am, I know that I *can*.

Because knowing who I'm meant to be, I know that I *will*.

———

This manifesto is open-ended; you should add to it whenever a new affirmation appears in your life. Remember, we are the authors of our life's success. That is both our challenge and our blessing.

Cherish the knowledge and energy that will guide you. Trust them and remember . . .

> **The path we take is sacred . . .**
> **The journey we take is shared . . .**
> *We* **are our own best destiny.**

ACKNOWLEDGMENTS

Many generous and wondrous individuals have enhanced the pathway of this book.

My gratitude to Judith Regan, publisher extraordinaire, for her faith in me. Her unlimited energy and remarkable fortitude create boundless possibilities.

My thanks to my editor, Cal Morgan, who keeps a multitude of balls (and books) in the air with deftness and dedication, for his fervent belief in the message of this book and the manner in which I chose to tell it.

I am indebted to the hardworking and creative people at Regan Books: Jennifer Suitor, Carl Raymond, Lina Perl, my publicist Beth Tarson, and the entire production staff.

My heartfelt appreciation to my talented and inspiring agent and friend, Linda Chester, whose enthusiasm and graciousness make my job as an author such a joy. She is a dream maker.

The incomparable Gary Jaffe runs Linda's office with aplomb

and handles all my questions and concerns with the warmth that is his hallmark. Many thanks.

My deepest appreciation to Richard Carlson for his illuminating and caring friendship as well as his remarkable and generous spirit that blesses my journey time and again. And to his assistant, Nicole Walton, who greets each phone call with infectious enthusiasm.

I am forever indebted to my dear friend and literary lioness Liza Nelligan for her astonishing insights and contributions that have elevated my experience as a writer and as a person. This book would never have become what it is without her discerning eye and caring heart.

My deepest appreciation to Dr. Steven Reiter for his keen understanding and psychological road maps that have helped illuminate my path as I wrote this book and as I've navigated the river of challenges in moving through my own wounds. He is a gifted soul.

To Debrah Constance, Kurt and Rosalie Bronner, and Steven, Larry, and Dotty Brody—my thanks for entrusting your stories to me and for your examples of heroism, faith, and determination. I am blessed in calling you friends.

I am grateful to Simon Wiesenthal for honoring me with an interview in Vienna featured in these pages. He is an inspiration to all who believe in justice.

My gratitude to President Vaclav Havel of the Czech Republic for the kindness of sharing with me his thoughts on the communal wound the world suffered on September 11, 2001.

I am so thankful to Lili and Jon Bosse, whose support and enthusiasm for my books and my family embody friendship. They teach me, in word and deed, that we are not alone and define what it means to make a difference in this world.

My continued love to Graham Becker, who has been by my side for years and whose contributions to promotional matters for my books are far beyond the call of duty. Graham and his wife, Lori, honor me with their friendship.

To my cherished friends Dirk and Linda Wassner, David and Jocelyn Lash, Debby Berger, Shirley Levine, Jane Powell, Victor and Miriam Rivas, and Mel Powell—I treasure you all.

To Lee and Fred Silton, Jack and Pearl Brown Berman, Jonathan and Rita Lynn, and Fredi Friedman for insights at the genesis of this book, and to all my friends at the Heschel Day School, Shofar Synagogue, and A Place Called Home, my sincere appreciation.

My deep gratitude to Loren Judaken, who shares so much joy with my family and whose love is a constant in our lives.

My brothers Michael and Mark and their families, and my sister, Ethel, and her family, along with my brother-in-law Glenn and his wife, Linda, all share in the encouragement that comes from a loving family.

My adult children, Yaffa, Batsheva, and Elisha, lived the lessons of Sacred Wounds with me. I couldn't have asked for better company or for more love and support than that which they gave and continue to give to me. Their success as compassionate and creative human beings is the source of unlimited pride.

I am blessed with two caring sons-in-law, Andy and Chris, who give me continued encouragement in my work and my writing.

My younger children, Ari and Shira, make success a living dynamic. Ari, at thirteen, is preparing a path to the NBA. Shira, at two, is teaching her old dad new tricks on a daily basis. All of my children, along with my grandchildren, Asher, Isabella, and Chaz, bless me with the sweeping possibilities of tomorrow.

The ability to write comes to me by way of my remarkable poet of a mother, Roberta. My theatricality is the gift of my late father, Frank. Together they have given me a belief in myself and taught me to go in search of my destiny, and to ever build on my roots. I cherish them always.

My mother-in-law, noted psychotherapist Dr. Marion Solomon, encouraged me to dig deeper in understanding the role of past hurts in our lives. (And she gifted me with the title!) My father-in-law, Dr. Matt Solomon, regaled me with insights on bike rides and in e-mail. I am so appreciative of their many offerings of the mind and of the heart.

In the end, there is one inspiration that soars above the rest. My wife, Bonnie, infuses my life with sacred joy. My ability to succeed is made manifest in her endless devotion to our marriage and our dreams. She is at once the greatest fan of my writing and the most determined to see it triumph. She is a wondrous and creative mother, wife, and amazing psychologist whose suggestions always push me closer to the truth. What more could any partner wish for? I carry her heart in my heart.